— THE POWER OF —
ECSTATIC TRANCE

"Nick Brink, Ph.D., has done a marvelous job translating and updating the work of Felicitas Goodman into our current times. In doing so, he makes indigenous wisdom more available to us all. How fascinating that the mind-body-spirit connection should work in all directions—that body postures can produce emotional and spiritual states of being! In explaining this, Nick Brink returns spirituality to the body—where it began."

LEWIS MEHL-MADRONA, M.D., PH.D.,
CERTIFIED IN FAMILY PRACTICE, GERIATRICS,
AND PSYCHIATRY AND AUTHOR OF *NARRATIVE MEDICINE*

"Nicholas Brink's book takes a big step forward for publications in the field of ecstatic trance postures. The heart of his book revolves around stories of healing produced by the unconscious while in posture. This book is accessible and informative to the public and a must for professionals in the mental health field, people engaged in alternative health practices, and students of shamanism."

LISA N. WOODSIDE, PH.D., PROFESSOR OF HUMANITIES EMERITA,
HOLY FAMILY UNIVERSITY, AND CERTIFIED TEACHER OF
ECSTATIC TRANCE POSTURES

"A few decades ago the topic of consciousness had all but disappeared from mainstream literature in psychology and psychiatry. Now there is a plethora of books on the topic, but *The Power of Ecstatic Trance* is the most unique. Nicholas Brink, Ph.D., takes his readers on a ride from the rituals of indigenous people to the laboratories of neuroscience researchers. Case studies and anthropological research add authority to Brink's prescriptions, while the illustrations and the detailed directions make these esoteric rituals reader friendly."

STANLEY KRIPPNER, PH.D., COAUTHOR OF
DEMYSTIFYING SHAMANS AND THEIR WORLD

"Nick Brink is a brave guide into the alternate reality of ecstatic trance. From his vantage point as a longtime therapist and teacher, he brings both wisdom and a sense of adventure to the journey to the Spirits. I've so enjoyed learning from his deep insight and open heart."

ILEEN ROOT, PH.D., DEPTH PSYCHOLOGIST AND CREATIVITY, CAREER, AND LIFE-TRANSITIONS COUNSELOR

"A must read for contemporary students of consciousness!"

STEPHEN LARSEN, PH.D., LMHC, BCIA-EEG, PROFESSOR EMERITUS OF PSYCHOLOGY AT SUNY ULSTER AND AUTHOR OF *THE NEUROFEEDBACK SOLUTION*

"As a psychologist, Nick Brink shows how this work with trance states lends itself so readily, gently, and yet powerfully to self-understanding and actualization."

LAURA LEE, DIRECTOR OF THE VISIONEERING PROJECT OF CUYAMUNGUE, THE FELICITAS D. GOODMAN INSTITUTE

"This is the best summary of trance work now being published. I am often looking for resources to suggest to my own colleagues and students, those of us studying and using ecstatic trance states. Nick's book will be among the handful I will immediately recommend to any interested in the personal and communal power of the human capacity to heal and to shift the direction of our life paths."

REV. JAMES LAWER, CERTIFIED INSTRUCTOR AT THE CUYAMUNGUE INSTITUTE

"In our overly rational world, body, imagination, and spirit are too often treated as if they are separate. In this fascinating and practical exploration of meditation with intentional body postures, Nick Brink opens a way for us to discover the particular and deeper experiences of healing and wisdom."

TOM LANE, FOUNDER OF JOURNEY CONFERENCES

— THE POWER OF —
ECSTATIC TRANCE

Practices for Healing, Spiritual Growth, and Accessing the Universal Mind

NICHOLAS E. BRINK, Ph.D.

Bear & Company
Rochester, Vermont • Toronto, Canada

Bear & Company
One Park Street
Rochester, Vermont 05767
www.BearandCompanyBooks.com

Text stock is SFI certified

Bear & Company is a division of Inner Traditions International

Library of Congress Cataloging-in-Publication Data

Brink, Nicholas E., 1939–
  The power of ecstatic trance : practices for healing, spiritual growth, and
accessing the universal mind / Nicholas E. Brink.
      p. cm.
  Includes bibliographical references and index.
  Summary: "A guide to ecstatic trance for spiritual and emotional development,
spirit journeying, and connection to the collective unconscious"—Provided by
publisher.
  ISBN 978-1-59143-152-7 (print) — ISBN 978-1-59143-829-8 (e-book)
  1. Ecstasy. 2. Trance. I. Title.
  BL626.B75 2013
  204'.2—dc23
                                                      2012035083

Printed and bound in the United States by Lake Book Manufacturing, Inc.
The text stock is SFI certified. The Sustainable Forestry Initiative® program
promotes sustainable forest management.

10 9 8 7 6 5 4 3 2 1

Text design by Priscilla Baker and layout by Brian Boynton
This book was typeset in Garamond Premier Pro with Bougan and Agenda as
    display fonts
Illustrations by M. J. Ruhe

To send correspondence to the author of this book, mail a first-class letter to the
author c/o Inner Traditions • Bear & Company, One Park Street, Rochester, VT
05767, and we will forward the communication, or contact the author directly at
brinknick9@gmail.com.

Contents

PART THREE

Extrasensory Connections through Ecstatic Trance

List of Postures

Foreword

By Belinda Gore, Ph.D.

This fascinating book is based on the Cuyamungue Method, which was developed by my dear friend and colleague Felicitas D. Goodman, founder of the Cuyamungue Institute, a nonprofit educational organization founded in 1979 and based in Santa Fe, New Mexico, that teaches the ritual body postures of indigenous peoples and serves as an environmental and spiritual sanctuary. Felicitas was an anthropologist who remained vitally engaged in the work of her institute until her death in 2005 at the age of ninety-one. In her research, stemming from a linguistic exploration of the phenomenon known as "speaking in tongues"—or more formally, as glossolalia—she attempted to recreate the conditions for evoking the religious altered state of consciousness for her university students. It became clear to her that in ecstatic rituals something must be done to the body to activate what we now know is the body's innate capacity for expanded states of awareness. These expanded states are not necessarily mental conditions but rather have their roots in physiological changes that then stimulate changes in consciousness.

Think of it this way: The body is a computer, the hardware; our mental conditioning, our beliefs and attitudes that come from culture, early life experiences, and personality orientation, comprise the software. The outcome of the interaction between the hardware and the software is our state of consciousness—what we perceive and how we respond to our perceptions, both emotionally and behaviorally. Changes to either the hardware or the software can change our state of consciousness.

We know about changing our bodies with drugs, thereby experiencing an altered state of consciousness. Those drugs might come in the form of a psychedelic plant or chemical, or a pharmaceutical such as an antidepressant or anti-anxiety medication. These forms are easily available as a means of changing our state of awareness or orientation to the world, but there are traditional means of altering consciousness through the body, including fasting, spinning (as in Sufi dancing as well as the spinning games children play), self-flagellation and other sources of self-induced pain, and sleep and sensory deprivation. Felicitas' remarkable and elegant discovery was that by holding a simple body posture while stimulating our nervous systems with a repetitive sound, we can experience a similar consciousness-altering effect, without physical side effects, legal risk, or financial cost.

THE SIX STEPS OF
THE CUYAMUNGUE METHOD

So here are the six steps of the Cuyamungue Method as Felicitas defined them.

First, it is essential to approach the experience—let's call it "the ritual"—with an open mind and a relaxed body. In this method, the mind is a key player in the ritual; it can trump the body, shutting down the experience—unlike drug-induced states in which once the pill, mushroom, liquid, or smoke has been ingested, the effect is so powerful that we cannot resist or control it. In the Cuyamungue Method, if someone is tense and unwilling, they can totally block the experience. Therefore, to reduce anxiety in those new to the practice, we help them prepare by providing reading material and reviewing information about the discovery of the method and the ritual they will be experiencing. For everyone participating, we initiate the ritual with smudging to signal to the body that the ceremony is beginning. Smudging is the use of fragrant smoke created from burning a natural substance such as an herb or resin. The smoldering sage or copal resin is held in front of each person, one by one as it goes around the room, with the invitation to wave the smoke over the body to cleanse the auric field and to inhale the fragrance, alerting the brain that we are preparing for a ritual and an anticipated change in the state of consciousness.

Second, we locate or create sacred space, a psychologically defined location that can provide a safe container for us during the ritual, whether we are undertaking it individually or as a group. A key element in the Cuyamungue Method is learning to surrender to the expanded state of consciousness. However much we may say we desire such a state, we have found that most people are reluctant to release control of their mental boundaries and open to what is not familiar to them. When we ingest a drug, there is no decision to surrender because the chemical takes over and does it for us. If we are not using a drug, it is important to feel assured that we are safe, so that it consequently becomes much easier to relinquish that control. As Nick Brink will describe in this book, a sacred space can be anywhere so long as a boundary is defined and that which is spiritually supportive is invoked. In creating sacred space, we call on the spirits of the Four Directions, the Sky World, and the Earth to join us so that their presence contains us, both literally and figuratively.

Third, Felicitas discovered that it is necessary to include a step for quieting the activity of the left hemisphere of the brain, the center of analytic thinking and language. Everyone has a nearly constant internal monologue or dialogue that is sometimes only noticed when, through some condition or practice, the voice in the head is quiet. Neuroanatomist Jill Taylor Bolte, in her bestselling book *My Stroke of Insight,* describes the remarkable changes that occurred when she shifted from left- to right-brain dominance following a stroke in a portion of her left brain.[*] In the resulting right-brain dominance she found herself feeling deeply connected to everything, in spiritual bliss but unable to dial a telephone or talk in order to call for help when she realized that a blood vessel in her

---

[*]For her personal account of this experience, see www.ted.com/speakers/jill_bolte_taylor .html.

brain had exploded. As a brain researcher, Bolte knew what was happening and is amazingly articulate as she describes the spiritual opening that accompanied her recurrent loss of access to the left-brain. In a less intense and dramatic way, we use a simple meditative breathing practice to loosen the left-brain dominance on our minds as we move deeper into the ritual. That breathing practice lasts only five minutes, but we recommend that people practice it on a regular basis at home to become more proficient in focusing on the breath and sustaining attention on the belly center rather than on the head center.

The fourth step in the Cuyamungue Method is the use of rhythmic sound to stimulate the nervous system and to cue the shift of consciousness. Early research on the neurobiology of ritual trance has indicated that multiple sound frequencies recurring at an even, steady rhythm (such as drumming and rattling) can block left-hemisphere processing as well as stimulate the peripheral nervous system, or PNS. The PNS includes the somatic nervous system, the autonomic nervous system, and the enteric nervous system. The somatic nervous system is responsible for coordinating body movements and receiving the input of external stimulation. The autonomic nervous system combines both the sympathetic nervous system that regulates heartbeat, blood pressure, and the fight-or-flight response, as well as the parasympathetic branch of the autonomic nervous system that compensates for the adrenaline stimulation of the sympathetic branch, causing things like slowing down the heart rate and the dilation of blood vessels. Finally, the enteric nervous system governs digestion. No research has been conducted using the Cuyamungue Method to track gastrointestinal changes, although everyone jokes during our workshops about how ravenously hungry they become after a few days of practicing ritual postures.

In the Cuyamungue Method we provide for rhythmical aural stimulation usually with one or more rattles and occasionally a drumbeat. Felicitas used the rhythm she heard at the Pueblo dances in the American Southwest, which is home to the Cuyamungue Institute; this is about 200 to 210 beats a minute. One of the institute's board members recently reported on findings presented at an anthropological conference showing that the rate of the rhythm is not important; we only know what has been effective and beneficial for the hundreds of people who have participated in our workshops, so we continue to recommend around 200 beats per minute.

The fifth step in the Cuyamungue Method is the key element that distinguishes this method from other practices: this is the use of ritual body postures. Initially, Felicitas did not include the use of body postures with the first four steps, and as a result she found that her university students did not experience the ecstatic religious trance state she witnessed in the small church in Mexico where she had done her field work. She concluded that people who did not share a similar religious worldview that included spiritual ecstasy could not move into the religious altered state of consciousness. Then an article on mudras, traditional poses for meditation, alerted her to the possibility that the body could guide a spiritual experience as effectively as the mind or a belief system. She identified a group of distinctive postures drawn from the reports of ethnographers working with small tribes and villages around the world, poses that seemed to be linked with some kind of religious ritual. It soon became clear to her that a body position, held in place during a fifteen-minute rattling session, could reorient a person from random altered-state experiences to true spiritual experiences. Felicitas began gleaning other poses from the artwork of indigenous peoples as displayed in museums and books; all the while, she continued to use research subjects either individually or in groups to determine whether a certain posture was effective in guiding the trance experience into spiritually meaningful and sometimes ecstatic states of consciousness.

In her first book about this adventure, *Where the Spirits Ride the Wind,* Felicitas began to categorize the types of experiences that might be the result of using a specific posture. By the time I published my first book on the subject, *Ecstatic Body Postures: An Alternate Reality Workbook,* we had agreed on seven categories of postures: healing, divination, spirit journeys, metamorphosis, initiation, living myths, and celebration. In no way were we suggesting that a posture was limited in its usefulness or that the people whose artwork had revealed the posture used it for that purpose alone. It was simply a way to organize a growing collection of available ritual postures according to the types of experiences the majority of people have when using them. It is also useful to know that if we want to have a healing ritual for someone, a healing posture would best serve that purpose; or if we want to support the spirit of someone who has recently died, we would probably want to use an initiation posture.

The names of the postures are our own creation, based either on an artifact that shows the posture or the nature of the experience that is typical in that pose. The Olmec Diviner posture, for instance, is from the Olmec culture, the ancient foundation of all Mesoamerican civilizations; it consistently provides an opportunity for divination or for asking questions. The Couple from Cernavoda posture is named only for the place the artifact was found—Cernavoda, in the Danube delta, in Romania—and for the fact that a combination of two postures, both male and female, are used together. We have done our best to remain consistent in the names we use for postures, although Nana Nauwald, the German co-author (along with Felicitas Goodman) of *Ecstatic Trance: New Ritual Body Postures,* and I both have confused things a bit by assigning different names for the same posture. In future books we will work this out. In this book Nick Brink has remained consistent with the names I used in *Ecstatic Body Postures* and *The Ecstatic Experience: Healing Postures for Spirit Journeys.*

Finally, the sixth element in the Cuyamungue Method is the ability to return to ordinary consciousness at the conclusion of a rattling session. It was Felicitas' desire to find a simple, safe, and teachable method to allow people to access the religious altered state of consciousness. The use of sound and posture meets all three criteria. When the rattling stops at the end of fifteen minutes, people are invited to move into another position, to sit down and rest comfortably for a few minutes. Stopping the sound and shifting out of the ritual posture are all it takes to end the experience. No one gets "caught" in an altered state, unable to return. Very rarely people may have a drop in blood-sugar levels, and for this reason we keep fruit juice available to help them get their systems back in balance. It is usually helpful for everyone to drink plenty of water during any kind of ritual or body work, so we encourage that as well.

Just as people need to record dreams soon after awakening in order to recall that type of altered-state experience, we encourage people to briefly write about what they witnessed or felt during the session with the posture and the rattle. In groups we share what happened, and then we may express the energy of the trance experience through dance and movement, through creating masks or other artwork, or through creating stories or rituals that combine our collective experiences.

ORIGIN AND USE OF THE POSTURES

A study of the ritual postures themselves is a fascinating undertaking. In some cases a range of postures has been collected from one group of people, such as the Maya in Mexico or the First Nation people of the Pacific Northwest, and compared to similar postures in other societies around the world. For instance, in *Where the Spirits Ride the Wind,* Felicitas included a map that records the appearance of the widely popular Bear Spirit posture around the world. We have also explored the subtle variations among all the postures in one category, such as comparing experiences from all the spirit journeying postures that have been identified. My own current interest is in how these ancient postures activate combinations of meridians and energy points in the body. The possibilities for further research in this area are many.

In the 1990s, two researchers published an article in which they concluded that since only a percentage of their subjects reported seeing a bear during the rattling sessions when they used the Bear Spirit posture, the method was not a reliable one. This kind of misunderstanding comes from focusing on content rather than process. The Cuyamungue

Method is simply a series of steps that activate our nervous systems' ability to expand perception beyond the ordinary, thus allowing us to connect with what has perennially been known as the world of spirit. We teach a method that changes how people's perceptions function, and then they have their own direct experience and their own content. There is no way to predict what the content will be, and that is not our purpose. We are altering the hardware, not the software.

The fact that the ritual postures come from indigenous peoples whose collective spiritual practices are currently termed "shamanism" creates another misunderstanding—that we are teaching shamanism. Though the practices are closely aligned, the Cuyamungue Method was not taught to Felicitas (or anyone else) by an elder or a shaman of any tribe or group of native people. As an anthropologist, she observed how ministers in small Mexican Apostolic churches taught their congregations how to go into the religious altered state of consciousness so they could speak in tongues, which is evidence that they had been possessed by the Holy Spirit. It is true that Felicitas observed closely and devised a method that matches many of the ways tribal religious specialists guide their people into the religious trance state. We are not proposing, however, that we are teaching shamanism; we are teaching a method for changing how people perceive in a certain time and place, so that the limits of their perception are expanded, thereby allowing them to see or experience what goes beyond the usual range of perception. When I was first learning the method, I described it as dreaming without going to sleep; this was more accurate than I realized at the time.

Dreaming is another altered state of consciousness, one that occurs during the sleep state. It is now commonly known as REM sleep, named for the characteristic rapid eye movements that first alerted sleep researchers to investigate the physiological and inner perceptual changes that were occurring during that stage of sleeping. As we fall asleep, our brain waves slow down, going from the mental concentration associated with beta waves, in a frequency range of 13 to 40 Hz; to the state of relaxation associated with alpha waves, with a frequency range of 8 to 13 Hz; and then to drowsiness and light sleep associated with theta waves, at a frequency of 4 to 7 Hz. Deep sleep is associated with delta waves, at an even slower frequency of 1 to 4 Hz. These changes in brain waves are relevant to our work with the Cuyamungue Method, as early research revealed that sophisticated subjects using the method showed very slow frequencies in the theta and delta range.

Carl Calleman, in his book *The Mayan Calendar and the Transformation of Consciousness,* identifies an amazing concordance between the frequencies of brain waves and the frequencies of progressive geographic and atmospheric spheres surrounding Earth's midpoint. He writes:

One is tempted to draw the conclusion that the different mental states of the human being are simply functions of resonances with different spherical layers surrounding the earth's center. When, for instance, we are in the alpha state, we are in resonance with a field of consciousness in the earth's mantle (extending from the earth's crust to the outer core), and when we are in deep sleep we are in resonance with the earth's outermost resonance body. I do not mean to suggest that the resonance itself is electromagnetic in nature, but rather that when we are in resonance with or when we tune in to these different mental earthly fields, electromagnetic currents with the same frequency are activated in our brains.[1]

Upon reading this, I began to wonder if ritual postures were an ancient technique for using the body to activate slower-frequency mental states while awake and then aligning with the Earth's fields existing at a similar frequency. Perhaps what we call spirits are the beings who live in these various fields. Animal spirits are mostly associated with the so-called Lower World or the roots of the World Tree, consistent with Earth's mantle—the spirit counterpart to the world of nature. No wonder people find inner peace, or move into alpha brain waves, when walking in the woods or communicating with animals.

There are other types of beings encountered in the spirit world. Some postures connect us with almost-human personalities, like the Lady of Cholula from northeast of Mexico City or the regal Mayan Oracle. Still others may take us on journeys to the Sky World, bringing us into resonance with slower frequencies, in realms further removed from material reality on Earth. Initiation postures can show us the mysteries of death and rebirth, possibly revealing how we might exist in realms further from our accustomed consciousness on Earth. We may have met them in our dreams, but now, using this method, we can know these different beings and interact with them in full consciousness.

All of these possibilities are explored in detail in this compelling book. As a psychologist and a dream worker, Nick brings his considerable experience in deriving meaning from expanded states of consciousness to the ongoing research in the Cuyamungue Method. As a colleague, his enthusiasm inspires me. I am delighted to introduce you to his further explorations in what is possible for we humans through this gift of ritual postures given to us by our ancient ancestors.

BELINDA GORE, PH.D., was a student, friend, and colleague of Dr. Felicitas D. Goodman, the founder of the Cuyamungue Institute. Since 1984 she has been deeply involved in the development of the Cuyamungue Method and has served as vice president, then president, and now director of training of the Cuyamungue Institute. She is the author of two books, *Ecstatic Body Postures: An Alternate Reality Workbook* and *The Ecstatic Experience: Healing Postures for Spirit Journeys.*

Acknowledgments

I first have to thank the several hundred people of the numerous groups I have led in ecstatic posture work who faithfully described in writing their ecstatic trance experiences for me to save, with special thanks to two who became central figures in my first group that met weekly, Sarah and Maria. Also during those early years and continuing today, I thank Belinda Gore for her openness in responding to my e-mails in an encouraging and at times critical yet helpful manner even though she had no idea who I was except that I was taking an interest in her and Felicitas Goodman's writing. I also thank Belinda for the use of her posture descriptions throughout this book. Her two books on the ecstatic postures, *Ecstatic Body Postures* and *The Ecstatic Experience,* are great resources. I hope I can be equally open to anyone who might read this book and in turn venture into the world of ecstatic trance and feel moved to email me: brinknick9@gmail.com.

I also need to thank Martha Ruhe, the artist who drew the book's illustration and Sabrina Kirby who read and edited an early draft of this book. Finally I greatly appreciate the staff of Bear & Company and especially Meghan MacLean, with whom I worked and who worked with me to bring this book to print. Thank you.

Introduction

For thousands of years, shamanic trance journeying has been used as a means of healing, of providing answers to questions, and of offering solutions that address individual, family, and community problems. Where these journeys take the shaman has been described in many ways: as journeying to "the other world" or "the world beyond," to another dimension, or to the world of "the spirits." In modern times this journeying has captured our imagination, as evidenced by the plethora of books that have been written about the work of shamans.

Among these many books, one in particular puts in each of our hands the ability to go on our own shamanic trance journey. That book is *Where the Spirits Ride the Wind: Trance Journeys and Other Ecstatic Experiences,* and its author is Felicitas Goodman, whose work we will learn more about in the coming chapters. Her lifetime of research into this subject has resulted in a body of work that imparts the necessary elements for such journeying and for attaining the ecstatic trance experience in all its power. Though traditionally it was the shaman of the community who went on such trance journeys in pursuit of finding the ways of healing and solving problems of his or her people, the work of Felicitas Goodman offers each of us the ability to go on our own ecstatic trance journeys. Many of us have been experimenting with such journeying over the years and have found it of great value on many different levels. This book is about why we may choose such an experience, how it can be accomplished, and what happens when we go on an ecstatic journey.

As a psychologist, I have gone on similar journeys for forty years through the use of clinical hypnosis and guided imagery, which in the clinical setting are used for healing of both emotional and physical problems. I believe ecstatic trance work has many advantages over the traditional procedures of analytic hypnotherapy and guided imagery. Trance is induced not with spoken words, as with hypnosis, but with the rhythmic beat of a drum or rattle. A practitioner of ecstatic trance does not provide direction through hypnotic suggestions, nor does direction come only from the unconscious mind; instead, direction comes from the body posture used and also from the world beyond, what we call the universal mind, a subject I take up in the latter part of this book.

The ecstatic trance experiences I describe are most suitable to a group setting, which uses the added strength of group synergy to enable participants to shift consciousness. In addition, the sharing and discussing of the experiences within the group after a trance session provide us with a useful understanding and direction for each participant. Each person in the group thus becomes his or her own shaman, yet I do not use this term in the traditional sense, as I do not heal others; rather, I teach others that they can heal themselves. We are discovering that we all have shamanic powers, powers that have traditionally been held exclusively by the shaman.

Though the synergy of the group can make the ecstatic experience especially vivid, the experience of an individual separate from a group can also be meaningful. I believe that for most beginners of ecstatic posture work the synergy of the group is important. However, at the end of a group session I have often suggested that individuals might benefit from using a particular posture at home on their own and such individual experiences have been effective in attaining the expected ecstatic trance experience. I often use various ecstatic postures on my own, especially the divination postures for seeking answers to questions, with good success.

To individually seek ecstatic trance the practitioner would most likely use a recording of rattling or drumming to induce trance. However, when I have been the rattler or drummer in the group setting, my experiences have also been meaningful and vivid, so sometimes I do the rattling or drumming even when using one of the postures on my own. I have also known people who have tried certain postures on their own based solely on the knowledge they gained reading one of the books on the use of the ecstatic postures, and the power of their experience brought them to one of the Institute's workshops. My one concern is that if people attempt posture work on their own and do not have a meaningful experience, they might go no further in their pursuit of ecstatic posture work, which is why I suggest the support of the group setting for newcomers.

Of the many shamanic postures that have been presented in previous books written by Felicitas Goodman and Belinda Gore, twenty will be discussed in this book. One additional posture used I discovered myself in the Branly Museum in Paris, the Jama-Coaque Diviner (as shown on the cover). We will discover postures that bring healing and ego strengthening energy into our bodies as well as postures that can take us on spirit journeys, whether to the underworld, the earthly realm, or the Sky World. We will also be introduced to postures that provide initiation or death-rebirth experiences, which involve the death of dysfunctional aspects of ourselves and the rebirth of more functional, healthy aspects. By using certain other postures we will also look at the role of the spirits of animals and other spirit guides in giving direction to healing and personal growth through shape-shifting or metamorphosis; and we will learn of the use of divination postures to seek answers to questions that may concern us, give us direction for the future, and initiate us in a process of self-actualization.

Beyond looking at the different postures and their immediate use and benefits, this book examines the purposes of the ecstatic experience more broadly—ranging from contributing to healing and solving problems of the individual, family, and community to providing access to the universal mind. It also examines the many influences on the ecstatic experience, including our expectations, the concerns we have in our daily lives, and previous experiences with ecstatic trance. I also consider those with little or no experience with ecstatic trance, describing what can be expected in their early experiences and suggesting ways to help them attain deeper experiences. Case studies are presented showing how these ecstatic postures and experiences can heal, and how they can take us beyond what blocks us in attaining our ultimate aspirations.

Finally, we will consider the evidence for the concept of the universal mind. Some ecstatic trance experiences contain information that would not otherwise be available to the journeyer through past or present sensory experiences, the common and expected ways we experience and learn of the world around us. These experiences, extrasensory or extraordinary, must then be attributed to the world beyond, what we call the universal mind. We will look at how we can enter into that world through ecstatic trance to interact with the deceased, with our ancestors, and with past lives. Experiences that come more clearly from the world beyond our five senses, including the mutual experiences of two or more participants in an ecstatic journey, will also be examined, as well as the ecstatic trance experience that can take us in the future.

Those of us trained as instructors of the Cuyamungue Method continue to discover and research new postures from ancient and contemporary indigenous peoples of the world. Using the body of information we have gained thus far, this book takes us beyond history and practice to uncover how the ecstatic posture and trance experiences can lead to healing, spiritual growth, and going beyond by accessing the universal mind. The intent of the ancient and contemporary shaman has been and is to promote healing and resolve problems for the individual, family, and community. The purpose of this book is to open the door to how these postures can be used by everyone to provide powerful individual healing and growth experiences, as well as to provide an understanding of how we can apply ecstatic experiences to our everyday lives.

PART ONE

The Ecstatic Journey

*I begin my journey toward ceremonies through storytelling.
When a situation or a person needs help, a story will often
emerge to entertain, to instruct, and to transform.*

LEWIS MEHL-MADRONA,
HEALING THE MIND THROUGH THE POWER OF STORY

1
Ecstatic Trance and the Modern Journeyer

Shamanism and the shamanic journey were introduced to the West in modern times through the writings of anthropologists in their academic study of so-called primitive cultures. They were read with interest and curiosity, but generally considered bizarre. These curious behaviors reached a broader audience through such popular magazines as *National Geographic,* but they did not reach a level of acceptance as a legitimate means of healing until the late nineteen sixties and seventies, with the onset of the New Age culture, and in particular with the writings of Carlos Castenada and Michael Harner.

Castenada, as a graduate student in anthropology at UCLA, wrote his master's thesis on shamanism, *The Teachings of Don Juan: A Yakui Way of Knowledge,* in 1968, and subsequently published two more books while still a student: *A Separate Reality* (1971) and *Journey to Ixtlan* (1972). In all, twelve books by Castaneda were published, two posthumously. Michael Harner's groundbreaking book, *The Way of the Shaman,* published in 1980, offered the emerging New Age community a way of attaining an altered state of consciousness through shamanic journeying, a form of trance journeying induced with the beat of a drum. Castenada and Harner have since been followed by many other writers, including, to name a few, Lynn Andrews, whose first of eight books, *Medicine Woman,* came out in 1981; and Martín Prechtel, whose *Secrets of the Talking Jaguar* was published in 1998. The continued popularity of books on shamanism and the proliferation of workshops and courses testify to the public's interest in the process of shamanic healing.

THE WORK OF FELICITAS GOODMAN

While each of these writers has shown the world the power to be found in the shamanic experience, it is Felicitas Goodman, in her 1990 book *Where the Spirits Ride the Wind,* who opened a whole new door to shamanic journeying by demonstrating the effects of different body postures on the ecstatic experience of the journeyer. Goodman was a Hungarian-born linguist and anthropologist, a highly regarded expert in her field. One of Goodman's early experiences while in graduate school at Ohio State University that started her on her journey of understanding the ecstatic trance experience came when taking an anthropology course titled Religion in Native Societies. Her professor, Erika Bourguignon, was studying the dissociative or religious trance experiences in 486 small, primitive societies to determine if these experiences could be labeled psychotic by Western psychiatric standards, a study funded by the National Institute of Mental Health. Bourguignon's study established that while such behaviors as having visions, hearing voices, and having contact with the dead may be considered psychotic by Western standards, they are considered entirely normal and part of the religious experience of 96 percent of these societies.[1]

From her early years in Hungary, Goodman recalled her anger and disbelief when she heard stories that the religious experiences of the Hungarian shamans were considered psychotic in nature, and that these experiences were forms of mental illness, schizophrenia, or epilepsy. I recall hearing the same beliefs about shamanism from some of my college professors in anthropology and psychology at UCLA, but my reaction was that of curiosity rather than angry disbelief. For me, hearing this was followed some years later by training in clinical hypnosis and guided imagery, training that began my forty years of professional experience in using these modalities to induce altered states of consciousness for psychotherapeutic purposes.

During the same forty-year period, my interest in the ways and stories of Native Americans grew as I shared these stories with my adopted part–Native American daughter as a way of helping us connect to her roots. Through the years, my interest grew, became even more personal, and broadened to include shamanism and the Native American medicine ways. Only in reading Goodman in 2006 did I recall my early—and since then rejected—belief that such altered states of consciousness are psychotic in nature.

Goodman's interest in religious trance experiences and linguistics led to her fieldwork in small Apostolic churches in the United States and Mexico, where she studied the phenomenon of speaking in tongues and the nature of such a religious trance. Her dissertation fieldwork focused on ten recorded conversion stories of members of two Apostolic churches in Mexico, one a Spanish-speaking congregation in Mexico City, and the other a primarily Mayan congregation in the Yucatan, where speaking in tongues and ecstatic trance played an important role in the conversion experiences of the interviewees.[2] While the vocalization known as speaking in tongues is referred to by some as gibberish, and by others as the manifestation of the Holy Spirit, it more technically is known as glossolalia, and it follows a specific rhythmic pattern independent of the speaker's native language. Reports of traditional people from around the world uttering similarly strange speech and sounds can be found throughout the ethnographic literature.

Goodman's research led her to attempt to reproduce such religious/ ecstatic trance experiences with her student volunteers in an atmosphere free from the religious dogma or belief that speaking in tongues indicates possession by the Holy Spirit. From watching the ways of the Apostolic Church preachers, Goodman distilled from their protocol some basic requirements needed to produce such trance, as mentioned in the foreword to this book.[3] In brief, these are:

- An open mind and relaxed body, along with the expectation of a pleasurable but nonordinary state of reality
- Sacred space, one separate from the activities of everyday life
- A meditative technique, such as counting one's breath, to calm the analytical mind
- Rhythmic stimulation of the nervous system through rattling or drumming

The stimulation with rattle or drum was offered at a rate of 210 beats per minute, similar to the beat of clapping and singing in the church. Goodman was somewhat disappointed with the initial results, not because her student volunteers did not attain an altered state of consciousness—they did—but because of the lack of consistency in their experiences. They seemed to be wandering aimlessly in their altered state.

Then Goodman read an article by the Canadian psychologist V. F. Emerson who, in his research with various meditative disciplines, "found that differences in their belief systems correlated with the fact that during meditation each discipline employed its own specific body posture. All the functions of the body changed with alterations of posture . . . the heartbeat, breathing, even the motility of the intestines."[4] With this discovery, Goodman searched ethnographic journals and books describing the shamanic practices of contemporary indigenous peoples, as well as museums for depictions in ancient art that described unique body positions that suggested religious ritual activity. Having her students sit, stand, or lie in these positions while Goodman shook her rattle or beat her drum for fifteen minutes more consistently produced the ecstatic visions and experiences she had sought to create.

Though Goodman's research into the phenomenon of speaking in tongues provided her with these necessary ingredients for producing these experiences, she preferred the more neutral term *ecstatic experience*. As she recorded the ecstatic experiences produced from these body postures, she found that particular postures produced specific kinds of experiences. In her book she presents about fifty postures that elicit eight different kinds of experiences. Some postures produced an experience of traveling outside of one's body, or spirit journeying, going into the Sky World, the earthly realm, or the underworld. Other postures facilitated divination experiences, providing answers to questions or precognition of future events. Some postures provided healing experiences, with some specific to women. Shape-shifting, celebration, and death-rebirth experiences were the other categories of ecstatic experience she was able to delineate. Since Goodman's original publication of her findings in *Where the Spirits Ride the Wind,* Belinda Gore has reduced the number of primary categories of experiences from eight to five by combining several of Goodman's categories. These five categories are: healing; metamorphosis/shape-shifting; divination; spirit journeying; and initiation or death-rebirth.[5]

THE NATURE OF THE EXPERIENCE

As an example of how Goodman's method works, I offer one of my earliest, and most powerful, ecstatic experiences, one given me by the Olmec Prince, a shape-shifting posture.*

> *9-17-07: My round black nose was twitching. I felt it as being more separate from the rest of my face than my actual human nose. My ears stood out, round and fuzzy. My head and shoulders were swaying back and forth, exploring—taking in my surroundings, using all my senses. I approached a tree and stood up, exploring the tree. Then my mouth opened and my tongue hung out, taking in even more sensations and smells.*

What made this experience so powerful for me was my sense of being totally "in the moment" for fifteen minutes. In the experience I did not say to myself, *I'm a bear;* I just *was* the bear. I have struggled through various forms of meditation and Tai Chi over the years in an attempt to be this present, but it has always been a struggle. The only

---

*An illustration and description of the Olmec Prince posture is found in chapter 8.

other time I had the control to be in the moment for any real length of time was as a beekeeper with the hive open and thousands of bees flying around me; in those instances I knew that if I squashed a bee they would all be quick to attack, so I had to be totally focused and aware of my every movement.

The content of the ecstatic experience can be anything from a simple sensory or emotional experience, possibly of a static image or picture, to an elaborate narrative of oneself or of changing into something else, whether animal, insect, plant, or inanimate object. In a trance experience the journeyer may be an observer of an experience from the past, present, or future, or all three at once, from ancient times or foreign places; or the journeyer may be a character within the experience. The journeyer may do fantastic things—fly, pass through walls and mountains, breathe underwater, or become the water or mountain itself. Yet, as simple or fantastic as such a narrative may be, it is invariably meaningful in some way, in terms of telling something about oneself. The experience may be very vivid, a separate reality, or it may seem to be no more than an imagined thought. During one of our group sessions, one person, who had earlier been disappointed that his experiences were so shallow compared to the experiences of others, told a very elaborate story and then laughed at the end, announcing that he had only made it up. Yet one cannot even make up a story without it being relevant or meaningful in terms of what it says about oneself. According to psychologist David Feinstein, "It is not possible to make up a story that doesn't reveal something of your own inner life."[6]

Native American author, theologian, historian, and activist Vine Deloria has collected many stories of the spiritual experiences of the indigenous medicine men of North America. In describing the nature of these experiences, he tells how Sword, a Lakota medicine man, describes the wide variety of possibilities.

Hanble (a vision) is a communication from the Wakantanka or a spirit to one of mankind. It may come at any time or in any manner to anyone. It may be relative to the one that receives it, or to another. It may be communicated in Lakota (or any tribal language) or handloglaka (language of the spirits). Or it may be only by sights and sounds not of a language. It may come directly from the one giving it, or it may be sent by an akicita (messenger). It may come unsought or it may come by seeking it.[7]

Thus the ecstatic experience may come in many different forms and in many different ways, yet as we dwell on the experience, over time its relevance eventually becomes clear.

Ingrid Mueller, a medical doctor at the University of Munich, demonstrated that the nature of the physiological changes produced by ecstatic posture work is different from the physiological changes produced by other altered states of consciousness, including hypnotic trance, REM and non-REM sleep, and meditation. Mueller's research showed that

> the blood levels of the stress-related hormones cortisol, epinephrine and norepinephrine initially rise, then drop dramatically during the course of the standard fifteen-minute trance. At the same time, the brain synthesizes beta-endorphins, which are responsible for the signature feeling of well-being that makes trance so appealing. The blood pressure drops, but at the same time the pulse rate increases, a rare combination usually associated with the preliminary stages of dying. Shamans have often said that they die during trance and these data suggest that they were well aware of what we consider to be sophisticated knowledge of physiology.[8]

Mueller also observed that "during the ecstatic trance the brain waves pulse at the theta level, about six to seven cycles per second, usually associated with deep sleep or the meditative state achieved by accomplished Zen practitioners."[9]

In another study professor Giselher Guttmann, psychotherapy science professor and vice director of the Sigmund Freud University in Vienna, measuring brain waves by direct current, found that in a state of normal concentration a subject's registered brain waves measured about 100 microvolts, but during ecstatic trance the person's brain waves were measured at 1000 to 2500 microvolts. This proves that the physiological and neurological changes that occur with the ecstatic trance experience have a powerful effect on the human body and are different from other forms of trance experience.[10]

THE VALUE OF THE ECSTATIC EXPERIENCE

Why are people interested in the pursuit of shamanic journeying? What really is its power? What was the value to me in becoming a bear?

Ecstatic experiences are often quite bizarre, just as nighttime dreams may seem bizarre and even meaningless. For some, spending time intentionally seeking such experiences may also seem bizarre. Belinda Gore suggests why we are so intrigued with trance journeying: "The ritual postures allow us to reach into our collective past to bring into consciousness this wisdom that is part of our human heritage and to integrate it with our present knowledge and understanding."[11] From my forty years of experience as a psychotherapist using dream work and hypnosis extensively, I have learned to value greatly the power of nighttime dreams and the hypnotic experience in providing people with self-understanding and insight into their personal lives, their problems, and their aspirations. However, dreams are often quickly forgotten upon awakening unless one cultivates the practice of remembering, while the advantage of ecstatic journeying is that the ecstatic experience of the journey is readily remembered. As for the hypnotic experience, the therapist has the responsibility of determining the direction of the experience. Whereas, with ecstatic posture work the posture provides the direction, and the ecstatic trance experiences map the progress of change in overcoming problems and provide the roads to growth, self-actualization, and creativity. The ecstatic experience can also provide knowledge from the universal mind (a subject that is more fully explored in chapter 11), which is not limited by linear time and operates beyond our five senses, hence allows us access to distant places, our ancestral past, and even the future. Understanding one's ecstatic experiences, as with dreams and hypnotic experiences, can promote and facilitate healing and growth.

Though the physiological changes in the ecstatic experience differ from those in the dream and hypnotic states, each altered state of consciousness is similar in its power to provide personal insight and growth. Each may reflect the processes of the unconscious and universal minds by means of metaphor, the language that provides the unconscious and universal minds their power. When a person commits him- or herself to change in some way, the change is real only when it becomes imbedded in the unconscious, when it becomes automatic. As much as we may say we want to change or will change, willpower alone is not enough. To become imbedded in the unconscious, change must be represented in a symbolic or metaphoric manner that resonates on the emotional level.

In my work I have experienced the power of metaphor over and over again. (A powerful personal example of the use of metaphor in how I overcame my phobia of using a telephone is found in appendix B of this book.) The metaphors of the unconscious mind are created through one's spontaneous imagination, whether from the ecstatic experience or from a dream. This spontaneous use of imagination provides the content of the ecstatic experience; as Albert Einstein said, and as quoted on innumerable T-shirts and posters, "Imagination is more important than knowledge." Psychologist Daniel Araoz offers a first rule: "It is not will that produces change but imagination," and its corollary, "Conscious effort of the will is useless as long as the imagination is adverse to the effort."[12]

Contemporary shamans, like the shamans of old, realize this potential for facilitating personal change by way of metaphor in their powers of healing. An experience reported by Sarah, a member of my first ongoing ecstatic trance group, who used the Nupe Mallam Diviner, a posture described in chapter 9, illustrates this potential.

10-1-07: I am running through a forest and after a while I notice I am being pursued. I then see I am the fox at a foxhunt, and the hounds are chasing me. I hear horses and riders. I am scared and running fast. I come to the shore, where there is a huge ship. I scramble onboard and we sail out to sea. It is rough, but soon calms—calms so much that there is no movement anywhere. The sky meets the sea without seam. All is white. I notice the ship changing to a large, soft bed. I am between white satin sheets sliding around in them. The bed turns vertically and I am sliding through the sheets out the bottom of the bed. I do not want to go, but I slide out and turn into a small, specklike piece of fluff or feather floating in nothing. Everything is white, and then I see a huge potato chip, which pumps up like an inflated pillow and it catches me. I feel safe and warm.

Though she felt threatened by something while in the trance, we did not pursue identifying what that was in our post-session discussion. It was apparent that Sarah survived the threat and found safety and warmth—an experience that demonstrates resolution of a problem and the gain of a greater sense of security by means of metaphor. The question may be asked, "What is this threat or problem?" However, since Sarah experienced a solution, answering that question may not be necessary, because healing occurs primarily at the unconscious level without needing to have our rational mind engaged. Since this was a divination experience—Sarah was asking the diviner, either consciously or unconsciously, to reveal something to her about herself—she may need to be on the alert for some threat; but whatever it may be, even if it is only known on an unconscious level, she has the reaffirmed confidence of knowing that she will easily overcome it.

THE FOURTH ERA OF CONSCIOUSNESS

We may ask why, since the 1960s and '70s, has the interest in the power of altered states of consciousness become so great? In his 1953 book *The Ever-Present Origin,* philosopher, linguist, and poet Jean Gebser—dubbed "the cartographer of consciousness"—describes how human consciousness has changed over the millennia: from the magical and mythical eras or structures of prehistory consciousness, the ancient eras of volvas, druids, and shamanic journeying; to the third and current era of rational, three-dimensional consciousness; and now, to the beginning of the new fourth era, that of integral time-free transparency. He suggests that we are currently in the process of shifting, from the end of the rational era, as seen in the breakdown of scientific methodology and classical physics, to a new era of four-dimensional consciousness, which is understood by particle physics and astrophysics as being time-free and transparent.

The time-free nature of this new consciousness is most evident in the burgeoning interest in the ecstatic shamanic experience as well as in modern physics. Whereas in rational thinking *A* comes before *B,* in the ecstatic experience *B* may precede or come at the same time as *A;* past, present, and future can become one. This evolution of consciousness explains the growing interest in such supposedly New Age areas as altered states of consciousness and psi phenomena, and a new appreciation of the power of magic, ancient mythology, and the experience of shamanic journeying.

Before the magical era would have been an archaic era in which people perhaps only had minimal awareness of themselves or of their relationship to the world around them. The rational era or structure in which we live began around 500 BCE and peaked with Leonardo da Vinci's three-dimensional art. As we now move into the time-free transparent era, or integral structure of consciousness, we see a return to our ever-present origins in magical and mythical eras or structures, with the integration of a deeper understanding and appreciation of their roles and benefits.[13] From this deeper understanding of the ecstatic experience, we have learned that anyone, not just a designated shaman, is capable of attaining and benefiting from the ecstatic experience—provided they are taught a reliable method. Such a method is the one taught by Felicitas Goodman and her successor, Belinda Gore.

2

The Unity of Ecstatic Experiences and Potential Influences

Fritjof Capra, in his 1975 book *The Tao of Physics,* attempts to merge modern physics with Eastern mysticism by delineating nine parallels between science and mysticism. I believe that the concepts Capra explores in his groundbreaking book effectively describe the processes of the unconscious and the universal mind and provide a key to understanding the nature of the ecstatic shamanic experience.

Central to Capra's thesis is the idea of unity: "The most important characteristic of the Eastern world view—one could almost say the essence of it—is the awareness of the unity and mutual interrelation of all things and events, the experience of all phenomena in the world as manifestations of a basic oneness. All things are seen as interdependent and inseparable parts of this cosmic whole; as different manifestations of the same ultimate reality."[1] A corollary to this is the idea that since the universe and everything within it is united, much is lost, if not rendered completely meaningless, if we attempt to understand the whole in terms of looking only at the parts. As Capra notes, "In ordinary life, we are not aware of the unity of all things, but divide the world into separate objects and events. This division is useful and necessary to cope with our everyday environment, but it is not a fundamental feature of reality. It is an abstraction devised by our discriminating and categorizing intellect. To believe that our abstract concepts of separate 'things' and 'events' are realities of nature is an illusion."[2]

That our society fractures the world and the human being into innumerable components and then tries to make sense of it all is borne out in our educational system, as exemplified by the typical university catalog. These hefty tomes divide and compartmentalize the human being into so many "departments," such as sociology, anthropology, psychology, physiology, etc.; then each department is broken down further. For example, within a psychology department one finds perception, learning theory, personality, motivation, cognition, and on and on; this approach results in the loss of the uniqueness of the individual as well as a lack of understanding of the person in the context of family and culture—the unity of that person.

Though true for all interactions between people, but especially important to recognize in my role as a psychologist/psychotherapist, the people with whom I communicate are unique individuals whose personality traits, problems, needs, and aspirations are intertwined, united, and cannot be separated, even while maintaining the integrity of the person. In therapy we may focus on one aspect of the individual, but impinging on this aspect are all the other aspects which need to be considered and addressed for fairness to the integrity of the entire individual. For example, defining people as introverted or extraverted is unfair to their integrity, because many other factors may determine whether they act in an introverted or extraverted manner at a particular moment in time. What I learned in college of personality traits and tests for these personality traits generally interferes with understanding both the uniqueness and the unity of the individual.

What is the alternative that recognizes both of these aspects, the uniqueness and unity, of an individual who is seeking help? The alternative is found in the stories or narratives that people tell of themselves that intertwine their many aspects or traits. For these reasons I value narrative approach and especially the writings of Lewis Mehl-Madrona. I discuss this briefly in the conclusion and intend to examine the ecstatic trance narrative more fully in the future.

I believe the most influential stories or narratives are those that come from within the individual, from the unconscious mind, dreams, hypnotic journeying, and now ecstatic journeying. The idea of unity, an ongoing theme of spirituality and mysticism in general, is thus highly relevant to the ecstatic experience and is borne out in the work of Felicitas Goodman and her successor, Belinda Gore. These pioneers in ecstatic trance work have considered the different components of the shamanic experience, such as the use of rhythmic stimulation with rattling or drumming, the shaman's posture with consideration for the effect of the body position on the overall experience, and the importance of establishing ritual to induce these experiences. The real power of the ecstatic experience, they have concluded, lies in the unity of all these and other factors.

Because of the interaction of so many influences on the ecstatic experience, the nature or intent of a specific posture is often not clearly seen in any one person's experience. Yet research on the postures by Goodman, Gore, and others over the years has shown that some postures tend to facilitate healing, while some are more conducive to spirit journeying, and others to divination, metamorphosis, or initiation—the five ecstatic experiences that comprise the core of this method. All five ecstatic experiences can affect healing, spiritual or personal growth, and will benefit the individual, facilitated by selecting the appropriate posture at the appropriate time. In future chapters we will examine some factors that might aide in determining the most effective posture.

Capra says, "The central aim of Eastern mysticism is to experience all the phenomena in the world . . . as manifestations of the same ultimate reality."[3] The same could be said to be true of the ecstatic experience.

INFLUENCES ON ECSTATIC EXPERIENCE

The unity of factors that influence a person's ecstatic trance experience may cause it to diverge from the expected effect of a particular posture. These other factors can override the power of the posture in directing the nature of the experience. I will discuss four of the most common influences on the ecstatic trance experience, which must be considered in light of the intent of any given posture. These influences include:

1. A person's understanding of the intent of the posture
2. The history of a person's individual experience with ecstatic experience
3. The various concerns and problems a person brings to the session with the hope for resolution
4. The other experiences, stories, and images the person brings to the session

In addition to these influences, there are many other possible influences: the influences of others in the group experience; family and community influences; the individual's personality, attitude, and beliefs; and the collective unconscious of past cultural experiences and even the motion of the stars in the universe.

Capra explains that the universal unity of gravitational pull is in the motion of the stars, the motion of the planets around the Sun in our solar system, and the spin and orbit of Earth; but it is also found in the energy fields that hold together the subatomic particles and waves of energy in motion within the atom and the molecule. These may be considered fields of wavelike energy. Rupert Sheldrake suggests these fields that hold atoms and molecules together and indeed the entire structure of the universe also hold together and influence the cells and organs of our bodies and connect us to the bodies and minds of others, holding us together as a species—he calls these fields morphic fields.[4] The pull of gravity on the postures, a pull influenced by far more than our immediate surroundings and one that becomes very noticeable because of the pain we often experience as we hold a posture for fifteen minutes, is one way we connect with these fields during posture work.

The Influence of Intent

Whenever I lead a group of people in using a new posture, I usually keep them blind as to its intended effect so that they can experience for themselves what that intent is. People new to ecstatic posture work are very often greatly amazed when they discover that their experience matches the intended effect of a particular posture, and with this realization they become excited about continuing in their work with these postures. Yet, in such a blind situation, the experience may occasionally diverge somewhat from the posture's intent due to other factors that override the power of the posture. However, once the posture's intent has been defined and described, their experiences begin to converge much more clearly toward the intended experience. After the experience I sometimes ask the person to again take the posture and ask them what they feel the posture is trying to express. The answer generally describes the posture's intent. The next time they use the posture the feeling of its intent is stronger and is more strongly reflected in the ecstatic experience.

Let's take a look at the influence of expectation as seen in Judith's Singing Shaman experience, (the description of this posture is found in chapter 11). The Singing Shaman is a posture of celebration that often involves spontaneous vocalization, the feeling of losing control over one's voice. Also, a sense of drawing the energy of the Earth up into the body is often experienced. In her first experience with this posture, Judith did not know its intent, yet she did experience the sensation of drawing Earth energy up into herself.

9-24-07: When I started this posture I thought, How will I ever hold this? Quite quickly I felt very rooted to the Earth, with my roots going very deep and long into the Earth. I felt my head grow tall, like I had a high view. I didn't see anything but became aware that my lower body was pulsing to the Earth rhythm from the roots. I felt the breaths of a large bird, and the breaths were like wing strokes. I thought the energy of the Earth was coming up in giant but slow flops of the wind/wings. I wondered if the pulse from the Earth was fatigue from my legs in the posture, but I kept the same posture as I came back out of trance and the pulsations, which had matched the drumming, stopped.

Judith's second experience with the same posture, once she knew more about its intent, exhibited even more of the energy of celebration—the vocalizing energy of this posture was exhibited first as a stream of energy coming from her mouth that was strong enough to ride, then even more so when she became that energy stream. This experience included the feeling that she was out of control, in the sense that she no longer associated with her own physical body.

1-14-08: I was a mountain, and I became aware that the breath coming out of my mouth was an energy stream that I could ride to fly to the stars. I found I could ride on this energy stream anywhere I could think of—then "I" wasn't me, my body; "I" was the energy stream. It was wondrous to think of a place and be there.

The posture produced great energy in these two related narratives, beginning with the energy that emanated from the Earth, but then energy that emanated from her mouth, strong enough to ride to any place of which she thought.

Sarah, an artist, and thus more right-brain dominant and imaginative, has a real gift for identifying with all the postures, and almost always finds their intent, even when meeting one for the first time. Her first Singing Shaman experience clearly exhibited the hallmarks of that posture's intent.

9-24-07: I am a huge mountain, very strong and hard. There is a very high waterfall running out of my mouth. The water cascades down my rock-body. I am timeless and ageless. Then slowly I transition into a huge carved rock sculpture, like on Easter Island, and the water stops flowing. I am all-powerful. Then I start breathing, and the waterfall starts running out of my mouth again and down my rock-body. Slowly I feel myself getting soft and squishy, starting with my shoulders and moving downward until I am so flabby I can hardly stand.

Sarah's second experience with that posture was even more celebratory in nature, complete with the vocalization aspect in the presence of trumpeting cranes and blowing horns.

1-14-08: I was in the jungle swinging through the trees on huge vines with a man and a woman (Tarzan and Jane), and we ended up in a tree house where we could dive off the deck into a pool of water. When we repeated this swinging through the trees to the tree house and pool of water, an angel came and blew her horn and made a lot of noise as cranes came and started trumpeting and dancing wildly about. Then it appeared that they were dancing on a piano and making a big ruckus, when the piano became a player piano.

Both Judith's and Sarah's first blind experiences with the Singing Shaman revealed the intent of the posture, but when they knew the intent, their experiences reflected that intent even more strongly. Knowing the intent of the posture increases the vividness of its manifestation. For example, if you are focusing on experiencing the intent this particular posture expresses, you might experience loud singing with great energy, closed fists on the chest with head back and mouth open wide. What is felt is the expression of both a flow of energy through the body and the potential for vocalization coming from the open mouth.

The Influence of One's History of Experiences with Ecstatic Trance

Another important influence on one's trance experience is determined by whether the person has repeatedly used that posture or other postures. In such cases, revisiting a posture may more easily trigger a return to the same or a similar experience as before, or a continuation of an earlier experience may be triggered upon repeated use of the same posture, sometimes bringing it to a more complete conclusion.

My own experiences in using the Priestess of Malta, a spirit journeying posture to the Middle World described in chapter 8, demonstrate how prior experiences with a posture influence one's experience when that posture is again used. While standing in this 5,000-year-old posture the journeyer will typically travel or fly to various places around the earth. Goodman speculated that when a person died, a shaman would guide the person's soul on a journey to visit the world in which he or she lived before leaving; entering into this posture provides a similar experience.

My first experience with the Priestess of Malta:

1-12-09: I tried to pay attention to my hand over my center of harmony, feeling its energy. I felt myself growing very tall, and after a while I felt small again—the roof had opened up and I could see the starry sky. I floated up into the sky, drifted around for a while, and then, feeling the chill of the night, I went to the full moon, where I felt the warmth of the sunlight reflected by the moon. After a while I drifted back to Earth, to the sunny side, and found myself in the jungles of eastern Peru. A village of native people welcomed me as if they were expecting me. I became annoyed with myself because I wanted to be with them, but I kept bouncing around, drifting off the ground. I kept drifting up into the air. I finally gave in to the feeling and ended up sitting on a tree branch, watching the dancing and drumming around the fire. It had become night again.

In my second encounter with the Priestess of Malta, I was able to start off where my previous experience had ended and the spirit journeying nature of the posture was even more evident.

1-19-09: I went right back to the tree branch in the village in eastern Peru. The women were dancing in a circle and the men drumming. I flew down over the heads of the drummers and dancers with a wand in my hand and tapped each person on the head, and sparks flew into the air. I then sat down next to a log and took up beating on the log in the rhythm of the drummers. Eventually the dancers serpentined around one of the women, and she fell to the ground in a convulsion. The rest of the women continued dancing around her. I felt concern for her and went into the circle and sat on the ground, holding her head in my lap and stroking her forehead. Eventually the drumming and dancing stopped, and the women carried the woman into a hut, laid her on a mat, and sat around her. I sat outside the hut, still feeling concern for her. At dawn she came out and smiled at me. A meal was being prepared. Meat was roasting over a fire, and I took on the chore of carrying wood to the fire.

The Priestess of Malta brought me back a second time to this same village in Peru, creating a more intense experience through repetition. In combination with other, more recent experiences, these two experiences allowed me to reflect on my role in helping others—a role that I have had as a psychologist for forty years and now have as a practitioner of ecstatic trance—and provided me with greater justification of that role. With repeated posture experiences, we are often able to obtain a broader or larger message.

The postures do not need to be the same to retain this kind of continuity from session to session. For example, I have three times shape-shifted to become a tree at the same place, on the mountain behind our house, the first time with the Hallstatt Warrior, a Realm of the Dead posture (described in chapter 8).

3-6-09: I went to the spot on the hill behind the house where I went before and stood, seeing activity under the log in front of me. This time I felt a bear behind me to my left and a deer behind me to my right. I stood there feeling cold, with the breeze/wind blowing from the southwest. I became a tree or was inside a tree barren of leaves, and I was listening to the other trees around me. I heard a low, deep sound—not distinct but joyful, a

sound of trees swaying, and as they swayed the movement caused the sap,
the sweet sap that nurtured the trees, to flow, and the flowing of the sap
felt warming and brought me slowly back to life from my winter dormancy.

Three days later, I was again a tree on the same hillside behind the
house, this time using the Feathered Serpent, an initiation or death-
rebirth posture (described in chapter 7). This experience was much the
same as the first one, only this time I found a squirrel nesting in my hair.
The third occasion of becoming a tree occurred several weeks later while
using the Olmec Prince shape-shifting posture (described in chapter 8).

3-30-09: I was back on the hillside as a tree. A weasel came from under
the log by the tree. It started wandering down the hill and out of my sight.
I wanted to see where it was going, and being a tree I could not move, so
I again shape-shifted and became the weasel. I wandered down to the
spring to get a drink. As I did so, I climbed over a log and got to the top,
but my hind legs were spinning like in a Disney Chip 'n' Dale cartoon—
but I realized that a weasel would be more coordinated than that, and my
hind legs would easily have traction. My body would be flexible enough. I
got a drink and wandered back to the nest, where two of my young came
out with their mother and started climbing all over me. I was then again
the tree watching them, feeling myself smile as a tree can smile. I was just
there and watching the world around me. Again an eagle flew into my high
branches. I was still struggling to know what it would be like to be a tree. I
wanted to be able to listen to the trees.

These three experiences marked the beginning of my exploration
of what the Tree of Life means to me, but the next experiences were in
different locations, times, and situations, where shape-shifting did not
occur. Through repeated posture work that produced related ecstatic
experiences, it became evident that the Tree of Life had become a spirit
guide for me and had something to teach me. Each experience occurred
when either my unconscious mind or the universal mind recognized

that I was ready for some new knowledge. The tree is me, rooted, yet reaching out, opening me to new vistas, a new direction in my life of teaching the ecstatic postures. In this situation, my history with ecstatic posture work was subconsciously influencing subsequent experiences in order to bring greater meaning to the experience as a whole.

The Influence of Concerns Brought to a Session

If I go into a session with a concern, such as having cancer, the concern is bound to influence my experience even if that is not my original intent. This is certainly true when there has been repeated use of the same posture. I brought my unvoiced concern of "what has been eating at me?" in dealing with my prostate cancer to an experience with the Jama-Coaque Diviner (a posture described in chapter 6).

> *6-22-09: I asked Jama-Coaque what he had to show me, tell me, or teach me. I found myself walking along a dirt lane, with a jungle to my left full of large plants with leaves like those of banana trees. As I continued along the road, I met a person with a donkey coming toward me, native-looking, with a broad-brimmed hat. Another man ahead of me passed him first, and they nodded at each other. As I came to him I nodded too. Soon I came to a building with a roof thatched with banana leaves. The building was to my left, and the walls were mostly open. I climbed the six or eight steps and went in. A man was sitting in the Jama-Coaque Diviner posture and beckoned me to come in and sit before him. We sat for a while, and soon a large black bird the size of an eagle landed on the sill of the building. I heard a voice tell me to watch the bird as it turned and then flew off. It soon caught a thermal and started rising in a broad circle, and again I heard a voice say, "Go with the flow" and "Rise above it all." I just sat there and felt the easy lightness in flowing on a thermal, relaxed and feeling in harmony.*

The eagle, whom I have visited on about a dozen occasions, is one of my spirit guides, yet I do not feel as close to it as I do the bear, or at least I didn't at the time. I cannot touch it or hold it, though I have shape-shifted four times into an eagle. The eagle, showing or telling me to "go with the flow and rise above it all," was telling me to rise above what was "eating at me," a phrase that often describes the nature of cancer (see chapter 10 for more on my experience with the eagle). In response to my initial question of what the diviner had to show, tell, or teach me, either my own unconscious mind or the universal mind recognized that I was again ready to or needed to face the very personal issue of my cancer eating at me.

I entered my next experience with the Jama-Coaque Diviner a week later with the feeling of this emotional detachment that the eagle had taught me, yet I wished I could feel physically closer to the eagle as I did the bear, a feeling or concern I brought to this next experience.

> *6-30-09: It took a while to focus, but I eventually went back to Ecuador, and to Jama-Coaque. The eagle flew back into the room and sat on a perch between me and the shaman. After a few minutes of watching and appreciating the eagle, the shaman pushed the perch over to me to where the eagle's face was close to my face and we were breathing together. I found a new closeness, a new strength that added to my strength in facing my cancer, more fully integrating the sense of detachment being taught to me by the eagle.*

The Influence of Experiences, Stories, and Images

Sometimes we are exposed to powerful images and stories in our daily lives that can influence our ecstatic experience just as they can influence our nighttime dreaming. Even our dreams themselves can influence our ecstatic experiences and vice-versa. In one ecstatic experience, Marty wondered if a movie she had seen the night before, *Narnia,* which features caves, waterfalls, and lions, had unduly influenced her ecstatic experience with the Hallstatt Warrior posture.

12-16-10: Waterfall heard to my right side. Upon more careful listening, waterfall was surrounding me. I turned to the waterfall, saw an antlered deer with beautiful eyes. Its head was protruding from the waterfall. It seemed to be beckoning me to follow it. I hesitated a bit, but then walked through the waterfall, which seems like I was going into the mouth of the Earth—red and dark, looking down spinning trees, loosening roots from ground to free themselves. Another pristine waterfall started flowing in the place where the roots had been. I jumped into the waterfall, and as I got to the bottom I hit dry land, but the waterfall was still there. There was a hand that was clawing and clinging onto something, holding on for dear life to this "thing." Surrounding the hand clinging to the thing was a bunch of lions, and they were chewing on a rope or something. It was one rope shared by the lions. It could be that when they were chewing the rope fell apart, and this caused the hand to release the "thing" it had in its grip, and then the water started flowing up the waterfall, beautiful bright colors. I was part of witnessing the colors going up to the next level.

I assured Marty that though elements from the movie might have appeared in her experience, it was nevertheless her own story and was relevant and important to her, and those life experiences that arose in her ecstatic experience reflected in an important way the issues of concern to her. With the intertwining and unity of all things, she chose to see the movie, the movie chose her to watch it, she chose to bring these movie elements into her experience, and the elements chose her. Such influences cannot be separated, the directions of influence often cannot not be determined, and together these experiences have an effect on her life. She was quick to realize that this death-rebirth experience was reflecting an important change that was going on in her life: she had recently left nursing and had taken classes in holistic health. She has since graduated from that program and has started her own healing-arts center out of her home.

Images and experiences from one's everyday life commonly influence the ecstatic experience. They are part of the unity of life whether good, bad, or neutral. A week or so before this next experience I had taken two of my grandchildren to Penn's Cave, in central Pennsylvania, a water cave through which visitors travel by boat. When I next used the Sami posture (described in chapter 8) for journeying into the under-world, I entered it through Penn's Cave.

9-10-07: I was floating down through a gray, soupy, thick, Jell-O-like environment. There was water below me, but I didn't want to go into the water. I went into a water cave, still above the water. It was Penn's Cave, and I went through and out the other side into the lake, over the dam and down a ravine to a campfire. I had never before been in this area of the valley in which I live. I was then lying on the ground near the fire with drummers nearby.

This early ecstatic experience, influenced by my family visit to Penn's cave, offered me reassurance that there are more like-minded people in our valley and that our small group is not alone in our experi-ences of this alternate reality.

CULTIVATING PATIENCE, GENTLENESS, AND CURIOSITY

In considering these influences on a person's ecstatic experience, along with all the other individual, cultural, and universal influences, any dif-ficulty a journeyer may experience in determining the purpose or effect of a particular posture becomes understandable. Although the unity of all these influences may cause us unease, they also bring us to health and growth toward self-actualization. The stories or narratives that affect our lives, especially those ecstatic narratives that come from our unconscious and universal minds, can heal us and take us beyond our unease.

In experiencing a posture, we attempt to exercise control over the various influences by holding the posture with intent—whether it is used for healing, divination, spirit journeying, metamorphosis, or initiation. In holding the posture, we physically/kinesthetically experience what it expresses, we experience its intent, whether conscious or unconscious. I believe that *intent* is the operative term. We may also enter any given ecstatic experience with a personal intent, often the intent of resolving some issue or healing some problem. We hold the question in our mind with intent and with an attitude of patience, gentleness, and curiosity.

This attitude of patience, gentleness, and curiosity brings us to the concept of emptiness and form.[5] From quantum physics we learn that matter cannot be separated from its field of energy, and from cosmic physics we learn that the planets cannot be separated from their gravitational field or void. From Eastern philosophy, we learn that "emptiness is the essence of all forms and the source of all life."[6] The way to find the answer to the question we hold, our intent, is to empty our mind, to hold the question in the void with patience, gentleness, and curiosity. With this frame of mind and with the induction of the trance state using rattling or drumming, we are led to empty our mind of everything but the energy of intent. From this energy of intent that we hold in our emptiness, we are given the answer.

Thus this attitude of patience, gentleness, and curiosity, along with focused intent, limits the interference of other influences, while the rattling, drumming, and purpose of the posture further focus one's consciousness in the ecstatic trance experience to open us to the answer we seek or the answer that seeks us. As we will see in greater detail in our discussion of the universal mind in chapter 12, we then can open ourselves to receiving answers from the universal mind or Akashic field, the field that holds our spirit guides and other messengers.

3

Initiating the Ecstatic Journey

Felicitas Goodman's six basic requirements for initiating an ecstatic experience are described by Belinda Gore in the foreword to this book. In this chapter we will elaborate on and describe how this protocol is employed in inducing the ecstatic experience in the group setting.

PREPARATION

Establishing Sacred Space

My private physical space where journeyers meet on a regular basis is a room in my home surrounded on three sides by windows that open to a view of trees, and it contains many artifacts, including figures in some of the shamanic postures, my medicine shields, and many of my bear and eagle totems. The journeyers have often commented on the spiritual feeling in the room. The sacred space at the Cuyamungue Institute in New Mexico is in a round, semisubterranean, kivalike structure with a door that opens to the east, and with the walls decorated with the masks of many trance dances. On the other hand I have on occasion used a sterile hotel conference room. The sacred space can be most any quiet space that is defined as sacred by the rituals of cleansing and of calling the spirits that follow. The spirits of the Four Directions and of Father Sky and Mother Earth are invited to join the journeyers, making any space sacred.

Intent

Upon entering the meeting space, members of the group are instructed as to the attitude and intent—the attitude of patience, gentleness and curiosity, and the appropriate intent to the particular situation. There are two levels of intent, first is the intent as expressed in the posture. There are times when we may keep a journeyer consciously blind to this intent, especially when using a new posture, but this intent is still expressed kinesthetically. In other situations, when we are working on other issues, clearly defining the intent of the posture is beneficial. The other level of intent involves the particular questions and concerns we carry when entering the trance experience, for example for a divination posture the specific wordings of what is being asked of the diviner is important to consider. The nature of such divination questions will be considered in chapter 6. Other issues of concern are often held in mind when entering the trance experience for any posture. With new groups or when there are new participants in existing groups, I begin the preparation portion of the ritual with the Felicitas Goodman story, a story that no one seems to tire of hearing.

The preparation may take different forms but often includes time for each person to express individual concerns or desires. Frequently this period of talk is facilitated by the use of a talking stick that is passed around the circle. The person holding the stick is allowed to speak while others in the group listen. When the person is finished speaking, the stick is passed to the next person, and so on. The group's teacher or facilitator then selects the posture to be used to determine the particular intent of the ecstatic experience and demonstrates this posture to the group. With more experienced journeyers I may encourage them to decide the intent of the particular ecstatic experience and the posture to attain that. For instance, as we will see in later chapters, a specific sequence of postures beginning with a divination posture and ending with an initiation or death-rebirth posture, when used over several sessions, can provide an especially powerful healing experience.

Once the decision is made on the posture to be used, I distribute pictures of the posture so that each one or two persons can have that picture resting in front of them. I will tell the history of the figure, and I may or may not tell the group the intent of the posture, whether it is for healing, spirit journeying, divination, initiation, or metamorphosis. Again, I often like to have a new group experience the posture blind as to its intent so that they can discover it for themselves. In other groups we may have a different agenda, and knowing the intent of the posture is important.

I then have the participants practice taking the posture. I check them as to the correctness of the posture and make suggestions, if any find the posture especially uncomfortable, as to how they might use cushions or yoga blocks for support. When all are satisfied with an understanding of how to hold the posture, we proceed with the ritual preparations of cleansing, calling the spirits, and clearing the mind.

Cleansing

To prepare for the journey, the leader typically smudges the space, the participants, and the drum or rattle with the smoke of burning herbs. In smudging, as one person holds the bundle of smoldering herbs, the person being cleansed repeatedly sweeps her hands through the smoke and spreads the smoke over her face, head, chest, back, legs, and arms. Instead of smoke, I sometimes use a piece of wicking soaked in the oil scent of sage, which rests in an abalone shell, and the scent is swept over the body in the same manner. This is considered an act of cleansing. Some consider this as the cleansing of the electromagnetic field around the body, and one person who does a type of bodywork and is sensitive to the body's energy field has noticed that the heaviness of portions of the energy field lighten with smudging. Others consider the smoke or scent of smudging as creating a doorway between the two worlds, through which the participant is to pass. This cleansing is an initial step in preparing a person for shamanic journeying.

Calling the Spirits

Calling the spirits of the six directions reenacts the Medicine Wheel story of the indigenous peoples of North America, a story that is central in the process of maintaining health, growth, and maturity. Rituals are "enacted story," according to Lewis Mehl-Madrona, a Native American psychiatrist. "We seem to be more profoundly affected by story when we enact it, when we feel the story moving through us."[1]

In ecstatic posture groups, the stories of the individuals involved are revealed in their ecstatic trance. Evoking the spirits of the Four Directions allows these spirits to give direction to the story. Who or what are these spirits? For some people the spirits may be considered metaphorical, in the sense that we use the word *spirit* to describe the feelings of a situation, for example the spirit of the day, or the spirit of Thanksgiving. Others see these spirits in a more real sense. For example, on the road from the Cuyamungue Institute to the hilltop where we welcome the rising sun, there is a spot where Felicitas Goodman saw the spirits of some native elders. In my earlier work as a psychologist I thought of such spirits metaphorically, but now, with my ongoing experience with ecstatic posture work that opens the door to more imaginative ecstatic experiences, these spirits have become much more real to me. As well, the concept of the universal mind has been described as a matrix of energy waves; these energy waves may at times be seen as spirits, thus adding to the reputability of the concept of spirits.

The story of the Medicine Wheel, the story of the Four Directions (or six, including Father Sky above us and Mother Earth below us), is a story of healthy balance. This story provides the positive and healthy structure that can aid a person in rewriting a dysfunctional story, thus providing a healthier new story or description of oneself. The story of the Medicine Wheel as told by Hyemeyohsts Storm, the author of the groundbreaking book *Seven Arrows,* is that at birth the infant's parents go on a vision quest, and the story that evolves in this quest gives the new infant his or her first story and name. This is the beginning of a lifetime search of the Four Directions to become a complete person, a person with the balance of east and west, of the intellectual and emotional aspects, and a balance of south and north, the physical and spiritual aspects. With this balance, and by honoring Mother Earth and Father Sky, the person finds the balance for a healthy life.[2] This story provides a positive direction for life from its inception. In contrast, the Judeo-Christian story begins in the negative direction, with the belief that we are all born in sin, a story that diminishes each of us throughout our lives. Another diminishing story is the one that so many of us carry: "You can't teach an old dog new tricks."

The story of the Medicine Wheel is not limited to the indigenous peoples of North and South America, but can be seen around the world. For example, in Northern Europe, the Celts celebrated the four seasons: Beltane/Spring, Lughnasadh/Summer, Samhain/Autumn, and Imbolc/Winter; these are represented by the four directions, beginning with west, then north, east, and south. The Nordic people also celebrated the four directions and seasons: summer solstice, autumn equinox, winter solstice, and spring equinox—the year's turning.

The ritual of our ecstatic posture work includes the calling of the spirits from six directions: north, east, south, and west, plus Earth/down and Sky/up. In calling the spirits, we offer them gifts of thanks, such as blue cornmeal. The stories that are revealed in our ecstatic journeying evolve under the direction of these spirits and provide the person with a story of balance and completeness that leads to health and personal growth. For the indigenous people of America, this ritual of the Medicine Wheel is central in a person's life.

The characteristics of each direction traditionally include a color and an animal, though the colors and animals vary depending on the traditions of the different native peoples. Though the Cuyamungue protocol does not identify with any particular native group, the animal associated with each direction is especially powerful in teaching, and a person's ecstatic journey often provides an animal spirit guide, teacher, or totem. Thus, in calling the spirits of the Four Directions, I highly value the animals traditionally ascribed to each direction and will occasionally mention the specific tradition, whether Lakota, Diné (Navajo), or Zuni, that I am drawing from when calling the animals of that tradition. I sometimes select the tradition based on my knowledge of the power animals that participants in the group have had revealed to them in past journeys. Over the years I have most often used the Medicine Wheel as known by the Lakota because almost all animals are represented.*

The rituals and traditions of the Medicine Wheel provide us with a positive direction in life toward growth, wellness, and harmony. The ritual center for the people of the Southwest is the kiva. For the Diné, the ritual center is the round hogan, with its door facing east, toward the beginning of life. According to Frank Waters, "In the kiva, man . . . is constantly made aware of the psychic, universal harmony which he must help to perpetuate by his ceremonial life."[3]

In my experience, psychology pays scant tribute to the four aspects of a person, the intellectual, physical, emotional, and spiritual, whereas the Native American Medicine Wheel brings these four aspects alive in a meaningful way. The Lakota Medicine Wheel places the intellect of the east opposite the emotion of the west, with the understanding that maturity is a balance between the two. In psychotherapy one regular struggle is to lead the client who intellectualizes to express emotions, and the overly emotional person to find strength in becoming more rational, thus seeking balance between the east and the west. Similarly, the physical side of us, the south, is opposite the spiritual side of us, the north; by being more playful and childlike, the essence of the south, and not taking so seriously what seems of ultimate importance to us in the moment, the essence of the north, we harmonize these two aspects. The Medicine Wheel, often described as a mirror of the human being, is powerfully dynamic.

---

*For a complete description of the Medicine Wheel, the colors, animals, and meaning of its directions, as well as its use in a therapeutic setting, see appendix A, "The Healing Powers of the Native American Medicine Wheel."

QUIETING INNER DIALOGUE

After calling the spirits, we quiet our mind so that we can enter the ecstatic journey with a sense of patience, gentleness, and curiosity. The Cuyamungue way of quieting the mind is to focus on one's breath for five minutes. I often suggest to journeyers in my groups, "As you inhale, inhale a sense of calmness, and as you exhale, let that calmness go deeper inside you." Similar techniques for clearing the mind are used in other traditions, such as yoga and Zen meditation. In the context of the ecstatic journey, however, focus on the breath takes on added importance, for it can also be considered an act of prayer to the spirits of the breath of life. According to Frank Waters, the Diné and Pueblo peoples, among others, believe that we have passed through three worlds and we are now in the fourth world: "The element of the second world gave (man) the breath of life. Hence to all the Pueblos breathing is an act of prayer." Waters further explains that "wind gave the Navajos the breath of life; their kethawns or prayer sticks are made of feathers, its symbol."[4] For this reason, one of the postures we use is the Toltec's Feathered Serpent, an initiation posture that is the personification of the breath of life found in chapter 7.

THE RITUAL

The five minutes of clearing the mind through breathing is brought to an end with the commencement of rattling/drumming to stimulate the nervous system. The leader or facilitator of the group rattles or drums rapidly, at approximately 210 beats per minute. The participants then take the selected posture. The intent established or defined by the posture gives direction to the ecstatic trance whether the journeyers have been informed of its intent or whether they are trying it for the first time and going into it blind. The enactment of this ritual in using one's body in a particular posture moves the person into the intended domain of alternate reality.

At the end of a period of fifteen minutes during which everyone holds the posture, the beat slows down for a few seconds and then the end is signaled with a brief period of very rapid beats. After taking a few minutes to allow each person to move back into the ordinary world of the five senses, the journeyers are asked to record their experience on a large index card or in a journal, after which each journeyer describes their experience to the group. Some discussion of the experiences then likely follows.

It has been my practice at the end of a session to collect all the cards, enter the information into a computer file, and return the results to the members of the group by e-mail several days later, with my comments and suggestions appended. My comments are generally in the form of "If this were my experience I might focus on what (a particular animal, image, or event in the experience) means to me, or ask, what part of me does that (animal, image, or event) represent?" This Gestalt technique often helps participants find greater understanding in their experiences. I often suggest that the person go back into the ecstatic experience with a playful imagination to let some part of the experience that seems incomplete go to completion. I have found that with practice it becomes quite easy to return to the ecstatic trance experience. I also suggest that journeyers observe their nighttime dreams, because that is where aspects of the ecstatic experience are likely to resurface. I have found that when group members receive my e-mail several days after the session, it helps keep the experience alive for them and often opens the door to greater understanding.

I have found that a person's ecstatic experience may not necessarily begin and end with the beat of the rattle or drum, but may start during the calling of the spirits or during the time of silence before the posture has been taken. On occasion the experience may continue beyond the final beats and may resume in a person's nighttime dreams. These experiences become part of one's life; they become part of one's life story and help reframe or replace dysfunctional life stories. In this manner, they lead to health and personal growth.

THE NOVICE'S EXPERIENCE

It is not uncommon for novices to ecstatic posture work to drop out because their initial experiences disturb their worldview or because the content of their ecstatic experience may seem to be so shallow they deny having had any experience at all. There are various ways to approach these problems.

From my forty years of experience in using hypnosis, guided imagery, and dream work in a clinical setting, encouraging clients to use their imaginations and sense of playfulness is most useful in leading newcomers to accept the value and meaningfulness of their experience. When hypnotic suggestions are playfully imagined by the client, trance is deepened. For example, the client uses his or her imagination when the following suggestion (very abbreviated) is made: "As you travel downward in an elevator, you will soon feel the elevator coming to a stop. As it comes to a stop and the doors open; tell me what you see." With deep trance, what is seen outside the elevator door seems to come very spontaneously, without intentional thought. Yet, the experience is no less valid or important if it is experienced in a more shallow state of trance, where what is experienced develops with a greater sense of imaginative thinking. As we have already noted, a made-up story can be just as revealing of one's inner life as a narrative that is revealed in deep trance. I have found that encouraging novices to use their imagination in developing their ecstatic experiences leads to a deeper, more fully developed experience.

A Group Experience with Newcomers

In November 2010, I led an ecstatic posture workshop for thirty-eight undergraduate students at Juniata College, for a class titled "Issues in Rural Health Care." The professor invited me to present to her class the concept of ecstatic trance as an alternative method of health care. I used the Hallstatt Warrior posture, a posture for journeying into the Realm of the Dead that I have personally found very powerful. After this experience I realized that this posture may not have been the best choice because the intensity and sometimes threatening nature of the ecstatic experience may have been one reason why so many of the journeyers had such limited experiences. I selected it because of the intensity of my own experiences with this posture, in the hopes that this intensity might mean the posture would be more accessible to new practitioners as well. Also it is a more comfortable and easy to use posture in a classroom where the journeyers only have a small area in which they can stand in front of their seat. This was the first time I had the opportunity to work with an inexperienced group of undergraduate college students. All of my other groups have either been more experienced in this kind of work, such as attendees at conferences on dreams, or have self-selected to participate because of their interest in altered states of consciousness.

Following the session, the experiences reported by the students were primarily sensory, such as seeing colors or feeling changes in temperature, experiences gathered through the five senses—visual, auditory, olfactory, gustatory, and kinesthetic. These sensory experiences were generally disappointing to the students because they were more rational, objective, and concrete than what they had expected, which was something more extraordinary and powerful, experiences that came from the unconscious or some extrasensory source. A more appropriate posture might have been the Bear Spirit posture that often offers the experiences of warmth and energy flowing into the body for healing or ego strengthening. Though this posture does not generally provide a narrative or visual experience, it would have been a posture that would have matched the experiences of many of the students of warmth and an energy flow, thus providing a validating beginning and first step in developing the novices ability in experiencing ecstatic trance. The Bear Spirit posture is also a standing posture that would comfortably utilize a small standing space such as that of my students.

Some of the students claimed to have had no experience at all but then described a particular sensory experience in vivid detail indicating that though it may not have been what they expected, they did indeed experience something. They reported seeing colors behind the eyelids, feelings of swaying, feelings of heaviness or lightness, relaxed or panicky feelings, and other similar experiences. A few students went beyond these personal sensory phenomena to experience something outside of themselves. These students claimed to have experienced the feeling of swaying, as in being pushed by the wind, or they saw in the colors from behind their eyelids some image or form that was from beyond their own personal visual experience. Of the thirty-eight students in the workshop, fifteen mentioned clear signs of trance by using such descriptors as "feeling relaxed," "feeling zoned out," "feeling a distortion in time," or "feeling out of control." However, while only fifteen students clearly indicated that they had been in a trance state, it is likely that most of the other students had also experienced some degree of trance as well.

As I typically do, I had the students describe their experiences in writing on 5 x 8 index cards. I collected these cards and entered the information in a computer file, to later e-mail each person his or her experience with my comments appended. For those students who had had primarily a sensory experience, I suggested using the imagination to go beyond the senses to describe where the sensory input came from. For example, if someone had experienced swaying, I suggested imagining what source was pushing the person into the swaying motion. If the student had felt heat, where did that warmth come from? If someone had seen colors, where did the colors come from, or could the person allow the colors to form a mental picture?

For the one person who claimed to have had no experience at all, I saw two possibilities: If that person's experience was truly of nothing, that is, he had a blank mind or no thoughts, he could have been in the state of cosmic consciousness, the powerfully relaxed state of transcendental meditation. On the other hand, he could have been having many thoughts that were indicative of ordinary consciousness—indicating meaning through the unity of his experience, or possibly he had resisted the trance state altogether.

Questioning people with regard to their physical sensations or experiences can lead them to recognize a deeper sensory level of experience. One student reported, "My experience was simple: I just focused on breathing, tried to rid my mind of extraneous thoughts. I mainly just saw fluid, light-filled colors on my eyelids: blues/purples, oranges/reds. Sometimes I experienced a tunnel. The colors were fluid, always-moving color groups slowly changing into another color grouping. Sometimes I felt a very heavy weight." I e-mailed the student the following response: "The experience of a tunnel could have been an opening to an extrasensory experience. By letting go and journeying into the tunnel, your experience could have taken you into the world beyond. What caused the feeling of a heavy weight? Let your imagination go. Let the colors you see develop into moving images. I would suggest that as you read this, you close your eyes and go back to the experience to see what you see in going through the tunnel, or what pictures the colors develop into."

Some degree of trance can be quickly revisited by going back into the experience in this way. Although the trance may not be as deep as before, the conscious aspect of reentering the experience allows a person to discover the acceptability of using one's imagination.

Another sensory example that became extrasensory: "The noise of the rattle distracted me from my own thoughts, and I completely zoned out on the rhythm. The rhythm turned into a steady breeze that pushed and pulled me toward something?" The phrase "completely zoned out" indicates deep trance, and attributing the experience to "a steady breeze" indicates the initial stage of an extrasensory experience. A suggestion that could take the person even further beyond the sensory experience to something extrasensory, would be: "Let go and use your imagination to let the breeze take you toward that something. Discover what that something could be." Again, using one's imagination can open the door to a much fuller experience.

Another, much fuller experience:

11-1-10: I felt physical changes in temperature; felt the sensation of heat followed by the chill of coldness. My mind was not very clear; I experienced a sense of numbness and unfamiliarity and a lack of total control of thoughts. The most vivid part of the experience was mentally visualizing a large gemstone rise out of the ground as if to present itself to me. It was a white crystallized gem that shined with a black radiance. Any attempt to "catch" the stone was futile, but attempts to destroy the stone proved successful; however, the gem reassembled itself after a time. A second vivid moment was traveling on a missile fired from a jet fighter skirmishing across the ocean. One last experience: I seemed to have the ability to transcend my body and be able to travel across the room.

The following is the essence of the response I e-mailed to this person.

This experience included several clear indicators of deep trance: the not very clear mind, sense of numbness, and lack of control of thoughts. It began as a sensory experience with the feelings of temperature change, but then it quickly went beyond to become extrasensory. What does this experience have to offer you, or what does it have to teach you? If this were my experience, I might think of the gemstone that is not catchable but is destroyable, but then reassembles itself, as something positive in my life, something valuable I am striving to gain. Think about what part of your life that gemstone could be, something that cannot be caught but can be destroyed and then reassemble itself. Also, the experience of being able to travel or fly is a very powerful and exhilarating experience. What part of you is flying, soaring across the room? Is it possibly the same gemstone-part of you?

Here is yet another example of an extrasensory experience that could lead to greater self-understanding and personal growth: "During my experience, at first I felt as though I was floating, being swayed by the ways of the winds. Then I found myself on a vertical climb up a mountain near a waterfall." This student nicely moved from a simple sensory experience to an extrasensory experience, from floating—a sure sign of trance—to being swayed by the winds. By attributing the feeling of swaying to the wind, she moved her sensory experience through the doorway to the extrasensory realm, to something outside herself. Experiencing the winds took her to the mountain near a waterfall. She was on her way to finding where the vertical climb would take her. I might ask her, "What in your life are you experiencing as a climb to something as beautiful as a mountain with a waterfall?" She can then close her eyes and go back to the recollection of the mountain and the waterfall and experience it more fully to see where it takes her.

Other Novice Concerns about the Ecstatic Experience

Sometimes those new to ecstatic posture work complain that their experience was only of some memory. Again, I always reassure them that such experiences are valid and valuable, by saying something like: "For some reason, at this particular time, that memory came back to you. Can you find some connection with this memory to something currently going on in your life, or to the intent of the posture?" I often suggest that people free-associate on the memory or specific aspects of the memory, especially the feelings the memory triggers. Sometimes I suggest that the person close his eyes and go back to the memory, give it some time, and see where it takes him.

Another common complaint is that the person did not feel especially dissociated or in a trance. My own experience is that I have been using the trance state for so many years, and I am so accustomed to it, that it sometimes does not feel exceptionally deep. To such journeyers I suggest that the depth of trance is not of great importance, and with practice the person will find that at times she can go into a deep trance, while at other times it will feel quite shallow.

Another common issue among those experiencing the postures for the first time concerns the flow or lack of flow of the experience when in an ecstatic trance. My own experiences do not necessarily flow like a story, from the beginning to the end, like the story I might tell in reporting the ecstatic experience. Instead, my experiences tend to consist of brief repetitions that gradually evolve, with a little substance added to the experience with each retelling. When I think about my nighttime dreams, exactly the same thing happens: something occurs in the dream, which I repeat over and over again, and with each repetition something new occurs. Later, when I recount the dream, I do not tell it with all the repetitions, so it sounds more like a coherent story that runs from beginning to end.

A post-experience discussion of this nature is valuable in encouraging newcomers to ecstatic trance work to continue, and helps them find value in their experience. In the case I cite, with the group of thirty-eight students, discussion was limited, but collecting each person's experience and then e-mailing them back with my comments attached may be even more valuable because it keeps the experience fresh in the person's mind for a longer period of time. With my encouragement, two of the students took the initiative to organize an ecstatic trance group that met weekly for about four months and grew to a dozen people, with a majority of participants not students, but townspeople.

PART TWO

The Power of the Postures

Ceremony, along with the relationships and community that are required to conduct ceremony, provides a social structure in which our genes can be modified. . . . I believe that ceremony opens the doorway for spirits (spiritual energy) to enter the ordinary world to do work. The credit for healing belongs to that other dimension, with ceremony serving as a kind of transducer to convert our prayers and desires into physical events.

LEWIS MEHL-MADRONA,

HEALING THE MIND THROUGH THE POWER OF STORY

4

The Purposes of Ecstatic Experiences

My very first experience with the use of ecstatic postures was when I offered a four day workshop for one hour each morning at the June 2007 conference of the International Association for the Study of Dreams. With what I would consider the astounding success of that workshop, I returned home to send out an email to a list of a couple hundred friends who live in the area. About a month later eighteen friends came together in my home to practice ecstatic trance. After that first meeting, we continued to meet for two hours most every Monday evening for the next couple of years with a committed core group of about eight people. This group included a school teacher, an artist, a massage therapist, a nurse, a homemaker, a psychotherapist, and others who joined us sporadically. This group has evolved, with others joining us and some leaving because of other commitments, but it continues and now meets about every other Sunday evening, rotating through different group members' homes.

During our first year using Felicitas Goodman's ecstatic trance postures, our group followed the protocol of not revealing the intent of a posture when it was being introduced for the very first time. After the initial experience with a posture, we were able to discuss it with appreciation and awe for the power of the posture to produce its intended effect.

During our first few months, no conscious questions or requests were asked when approaching a specific posture or of images met in the experience. After those first few months, as we began to explore how these postures can be used, we began coming to the ecstatic trance state with questions. For example, at the conclusion of an ecstatic experience, while reviewing the journeyers' experiences, questions would often arise that would be asked in the next trance experience. For instance, when a journeyer met a new spirit guide, an important question to ask in the next journey might be "What does that spirit guide have to teach me." Even without such questions or requests, several members of our group found healing through their ecstatic experiences for such diverse problems as quitting smoking, overcoming the depression of empty-nest syndrome, and overcoming a fear of snakes. These persons likely entered the ecstatic experience with these concerns on their mind with some degree of consciousness.

Initially, we simply wanted to explore our ecstatic experiences and learn more about and better understand the postures and the ancient or indigenous traditions they came from. To facilitate this, each week I distributed illustrations of the posture to group members and told them what was known about its age, where it comes from, and what was known about the people of its time and place—information that does not necessarily reveal the intent of the posture. I generally offered the group multiple postures to choose from and the group would make the final decision. Then, after our ritual of cleansing and calling on the spirits of the six directions, we called on the spirit of the posture to join us. These posture spirits are what we sought to understand in hopes that they would open to us the intent of the posture.

Once a group has become familiar with using the postures, understands the intent of the postures, and is accustomed to entering the trance state, the individual members of the group are more prepared to use the postures to seek answers to personal questions. However, the questions we ask may be biased and carry with them certain expectations. The spirits we call on can free us from such biases and expectations and open us to asking the appropriate question to meet our particular needs and concerns. Such questions as, "What can this posture tell me or show me?" produce answers to particular concerns of the individual but will likely not reveal whether a posture is for divination, metamorphosis, initiation, spirit journeying, or healing. To reveal the intent of a particular posture we might frame a more specific question, such as, "What is the effect of this posture on the nature of the ecstatic experience?" or "What is the intent of the posture?" The purposes of the ecstatic experience range from identifying the intent of a specific posture to gaining broader understanding; from healing illnesses and emotional pain to overcoming individual, family, or community problems; from gaining personal growth and self-actualization to, ultimately, connecting with the universal mind.

I have found that certain postures are more powerful, or at least seem more powerful, for some people than for others. I expect a traditional shaman likely did not use a large number of postures and might have used only one or two. I suspect that eight or nine postures might be the maximum number that are useful for any given person: a posture for healing, one for divination, and postures for spirit journeying into the three realms and the Realm of the Dead, one for metamorphosis, and one for initiation.

The distinctions as to what these postures offer can often overlap, and the ecstatic experience can be influenced by many factors. For example, divination, using a spirit guide, and spirit journeying are all important factors in healing and providing answers to questions regarding the whys and hows of healing. Also, a shaman may prefer, and find it quite effective, to heal using a shape-shifting posture in order to follow a spirit guide in search of answers rather than using a healing posture— as was my experience. In my process of healing my prostate cancer, the Olmec Prince, a shape-shifting posture, and the Hallstatt Warrior, a spirit journeying posture, provided me with more profound experiences than those classified as healing postures; with time, however, the healing and cleansing Tlazolteotl posture gained strength for me as well. The spirit journeying posture the Venus of Galgenberg also provided me with healing energy further into my process. And while, when the questions regarding such matters are clearly stated, a divination posture may be most appropriate to assist us in making life decisions, most postures can provide us helpful clues.

The ecstatic postures can lead a person to greater personal growth and self-actualization. Such an evolution is seen over a period of time. For instance, Maria, a member of the ecstatic trance group that met weekly at my home, knew it would be hell to quit smoking, but her ecstatic experience with the Nupe Mallam, a divination posture, greatly abbreviated her time in hell and allowed her to quit once and for all. After she quit smoking, she was interested in furthering her growth, especially since she had also just broken up with her man. As we will see in chapter 9, which describes how the trance experience can be used over time to attain self-actualization, during the six months following quitting smoking, Maria had a number of ecstatic experiences, each one taking her to a new level of self-knowledge and inner growth, giving her a sense of ease and contentment and enabling her to find a level of self-confidence and inner security that she had never known she possessed.

Traditional peoples went to their community shaman for healing, for solving family and community problems, for seeking ways to improve their success in hunting and gardening, for determining whether a particular plant was edible or how it might be used for healing, for dealing with what to do at the time of death, and for addressing many other aspects of daily life. Though we tend to think that only the shaman of a community has extraordinary powers, entire communities have access to this kind of power. We all have access to the power—that we may now call extrasensory—to seek solutions to life's problems. According to Ervin Laszlo, among traditional peoples, "whole clans seem able to remain in touch with each other no matter where their members roam."[1] Vine Deloria, in his book *The World We Used to Live In,* compiled many stories of the extraordinary experiences of the native peoples of North America. To offer just one brief example: "Siya'ka tells the story that he lost two horses. White Shield, using his way of knowing, tells Siya'ka that his horses were fifteen miles west of Porcupine

Hills, at the fork of Porcupine Creek. He knew that a traveler was coming from that direction and would return the horses. This proved to be true—a neighbor of Siya'ka had been on his way home when he recognized the horses and brought them back."[2]

When the daughter of one group member was diagnosed with lupus and the grandson of a good friend of several members of our group was diagnosed with a terminal brain tumor, our sessions became more goal-directed as we entered the trance experience with the intent of helping these members of our community—another valuable purpose of the journeying we do. The teenage daughter with lupus eventually healed and continues to be symptom free. Of course there was no way for us to know if our work helped in this healing, but the experiences brought us closer to her mother, providing her with support, emotional healing, and many hugs. Sadly, the grandson of our friend died a few weeks after we learned of his illness; however, our energy in reaching out to the boy's family and the images we received of him in trance, in which he was playing and laughing or sleeping contently, helped us all deal with the pain of losing him and assisted us in supporting the family in their process of grieving. The results of ecstatic trance work may not always be just what we expected, but it may provide unintended yet important effects such as bringing people closer together in mutual support or in grief.

There is a growing body of evidence that there exists a source of information beyond our human mind yet which is accessible by the human mind, but not through the five senses. It has been called by various names: the morphic field by Rupert Sheldrake,[3] the Akashic field by Ervin Laszlo,[4] the Divine Matrix by Gregg Braden,[5] and the collective unconscious by Carl Jung.[6] I prefer the term *universal mind.** Through this universal mind, one has access to all knowledge, known and unknown. It exists beyond our physicality and acts as a spirit guide.

---

*The term *universal mind* was popularized by the New Thought movement, which started in the nineteenth century to promote the ideas that "Infinite Intelligence," or God, is ubiquitous, spirit is the totality of real things, true human selfhood is divine, divine thought is a force for good, sickness originates in the mind, and "right thinking" has a healing effect.

This universal mind may be accessed through dreams and hypnosis; we can also tap into it through our ecstatic experiences in ecstatic posture work. Through it we can communicate with ancestors, with ourselves in past lives, and with others who may act as spirit guides or messengers.

We can be our own shamans; we can access our inherent human potential, for the benefit of ourselves, our families, our "tribe" of friends and associates, and even on behalf of the planet. This power is available to each of us, provided we look beyond our rigid, rational, analytical mind and open ourselves to the power of the unconscious and universal mind—a power that can be facilitated by the ecstatic postures.

5
Healing Postures
Healing Physical, Mental, and Emotional Issues

Healing is a primary function of the shamanic ecstatic journey. Though all of the postures may be used with the intent to heal, the healing postures are a logical beginning in this direction. Of all the healing postures, I have used the Bear Spirit and the Tlazolteotl most frequently for addressing issues that require healing on the physical, mental, and emotional planes. In our understanding of disease, beyond our obvious physical and emotional problems, we also include such chronic issues as poverty, ignorance, and other conditions that manifest as a result of imbalance. The healing may be for oneself or for others.

THE GREAT HEALER

Feelings of strength, warmth, and nurturance are so often a person's first experience in using the Bear Spirit, and these basic elements of love are the nature of its healing energy.

The Bear Spirit originates in the coastal area of the Pacific Northwest, identified and named based on a wood carving of a bear standing behind and holding a shaman—who stands with the body posture we use for this pose. However, this image can be found in virtually every area of the world, going as far back as 6000 BCE, and it is still found among contemporary indigenous peoples of many diverse cultures. Among my collection of totemic objects I have two such bear spirit figures that were carved by the San Blas Indians of Panama, who refer to these figures as dream figures. The figure of the bear holding the shaman is part of the logo of the Cuyamungue Institute.

The Bear Spirit cures disease and restores harmony and balance and thus is known throughout the world as the Great Healer. I find this posture especially powerful in providing increased ego strength, a strength that I, as a psychologist, would attempt to hypnotically instill in preparing a client to face some intense or traumatic issue. Similarly, a journeyer can be led to find additional strength by using the Bear Spirit posture to prepare for a journey through the potentially frightening images that might be found in the Lower World and the Realm of the Dead. In venturing into the Lower World, or psychologically the unconscious mind, painful emotional issues of past trauma may be faced that otherwise might be avoided without sufficient ego strength.

It is not unusual for participants in trance with the Bear Spirit to experience being split open or dismembered; this suggests opening to receive the free flow of energy of one form or another from outside oneself or from within, a healing energy that can take on various colors and substances.

My very first ecstatic experience with the Bear Spirit was in 2007, with a group of attendees of the International Association for the Study of Dreams Conference in Sonoma, California. All those who participated in this posture did so without knowing its intent, and afterward they reported their experiences on a 5 x 8 index card. Because of their interest in and sensitivity to altered states of consciousness such as dreams, not unexpectedly, most of the journeyers experienced the posture's expected intent in feeling its flowing energy. In my first experience with this posture, I noted: "Great warmth in my belly—warmth spreading from my feet upward. The drumming moved to inside my head. Then I started hearing the drumming as

Bear Spirit Posture

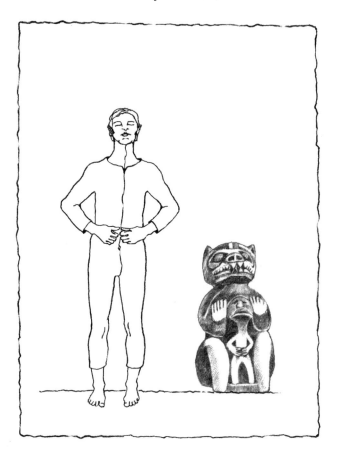

Stand with your feet parallel, about six inches apart, with toes forward and knees not locked but slightly flexed. Your hands are resting relaxed on your abdomen, with the tips of your thumbs lightly touching each other above the navel and with your fingers bent such that the first knuckle of your index fingers touch each other below the navel, forming a triangle around your navel. Your elbows rest easily at your side. Your eyes are closed, and your head is gently tipped back as though you are looking at a point where the wall meets the ceiling.

trash-can lids being banged together. I saw a bear banging around trash cans at a campsite before it came up behind me and hugged me. My arms and hands became the arms and paws of a bear. The hug felt very warm and comfortable."

The energy of warmth felt very healing though I did not know specifically at the time what needed to be healed. Afterward I could think of many aspects of my life that could have benefited by this healing. I had to laugh at the trash-can lids, recalling that many years ago while camping at Yosemite, I woke in the night to the noise of the bears in the nearby trash cans, another example of how the unity of experiences can come together in ecstatic trance.

The energy of the Bear Spirit can take any number of different forms. Another participant in the workshop experienced this energy as a liquid crystal ocean flowing from the top of her head to her mid-pelvis—clear, blue, and aqua. Back home, with the group that meets weekly, we tried this posture. Sue (9-3-07) had a vivid experience of the circular flow of the healing energy of the Bear. In her experience, Sue circled a campfire clockwise to the rhythm of the drum. After some time the energy shifted, and the focus of her trance went to the entire group, which circled counterclockwise—we know that personal energy circles clockwise, collective energy counterclockwise. As this counterclockwise energy expanded outward, it began to move in a spiral pattern; then the spiral moved around someone lying in a field for healing. The energy around Sue at this point circled clockwise, for her self-healing, while the rest of the group continued to circle around her in a counterclockwise direction. What Sue was trying to heal was not pursued and was not likely conscious to her at the time as she entered this experience blind to the intent of the posture. I believe there is always something the Bear Spirit can find that needs to be healed or strengthened, even if it is just our ego strength or self-confidence.

On the day of my prostate surgery in 2009, one of the members of our weekly group, Sarah, used the Bear Spirit posture to reach out to me with healing energy. The result was a vivid image very characteristic of the healing qualities of this posture:

5-12-09: I felt like I was holding a baby in my arms, and then I placed it on the grass. It slowly aged and turned into you. A white bear appeared and picked you up and wrapped you in a fur skin he brought for you. He held you to him with your feet dangling. The bear squeezed you, and a blob of organic matter eventually fell out of you. He laid you down and covered you with the fur and placed an amulet around your neck, amber, it looked like. He built a fire and it was dark. He picked up the blob of organic matter and threw it into the fire. Volumes of blue smoke billowed forth. Several small dark men came, drawn by the fire, and greeted the white bear. Then they all linked hands and danced in a circle around the fire, the bear, and you. They would pause, drop their hands and lean toward the center of the circle and wiggle their fingers on their outstretched arms. Then they would join hands again and resume dancing. Slowly, it became light out and the dancers went to sleep on the ground. The white bear picked you up and put you on your feet, and you walked home.

Though I was unaware of Sarah using this posture for my benefit at about the time of my surgery and from about 150 miles away, I appreciated her concern and support when I heard about what she did a few days later after returning home. This is one example of support from my community that I believe facilitates healing. In addition to her support, I believe that the positive healing energy Sarah generated through her ecstatic experience with the Bear Spirit likely contributed to my healing.

What and how does the Bear Spirit heal? On the physical level, the warmth that journeyers experience with the Bear results in increased blood circulation can strengthen the immune system. Feeling warm and comfortable can facilitate relaxation and sleep, which in turn facilitates wellness. On the emotional level, feeling loved increases a person's ego strength of feeling good, strong, healthy and self-confident about oneself.

For example, as I write this I am sitting at my computer with a head cold. My nose is stuffed up, and I am breathing through my mouth. I know that cold medications can relieve the congestion, which is only a symptom: the medication will allow me to sleep better, and sleep can be healing. The warmth and nurturance offered by the Bear Spirit can work in the same way, allowing one to sleep more comfortably. From my experience with hypnosis, hypnotic relaxation and ego-strength building have repeatedly been shown as effective in strengthening the immune system, increasing body temperature, improving circulation, and bringing better balance to one's life. The ecstatic experience with the Bear Spirit has the same effect.

CLEANSING OUR "FILTH"

In Aztec mythology, Tlazolteotl is the Mother Earth goddess, the Mother Confessor. In Nahuatl, the word tlazolli can refer to vice and diseases. Thus Tlazolteotl was a goddess of "filth" (i.e., sin, vice, and sexual misdeeds). The people take to her their sins, which she eats, then rebirths them to their innocence and health. For this reason she is known as a purification goddess who cleanses and nurtures by relieving the toxic wastes we are unable to eliminate from our bodies, or perhaps even more important, by eliminating the wastes of past mistakes, old hurts, grievances, and guilt that accumulate in the emotional body and can manifest on the physical plane as illness.

I was first introduced to Tlazolteotl in 1992, when I attended a conference of the International Society of Experimental and Clinical Hypnosis, held in Constance, Germany. It was there that I met Teresa Robles, cofounder of the Milton H. Erickson Institute in Mexico City. I asked her about the various religious traditions of the indigenous people of Mexico that may be relevant in the practice of psychotherapy and emotional well-being. In response, she introduced me to the Aztec goddess Tlazolteotl and said that many of the people of her country continue to revere this goddess and go to her with their guilt. A year later, Teresa and I met again in San Diego at a hypnosis conference. From there I took a side trip to Tijuana and purchased two figurines that Teresa identified as Tlazolteotl.

Most images of Tlazolteotl show her with a ring of filth around her mouth, squatting in the position of childbirth, giving birth to a baby, which represents innocence. This image of the goddess is the reason why she is sometimes incorrectly referred to as a fertility goddess. The figure of Tlazolteotl that we use for purification shows her standing (see page 63).

Cleansing is a central motif of this posture, and it can take different forms. For example, in my experiences of 1-7-08 with Tlazolteotl, I stood on a rock ledge above a pool as a warm waterfall cascaded over me. Then I dove into the pool, saw a salmon-like fish, explored a shallow cave in the pool, surfaced, dove again, this time deeper, and eventually came up to rest on the ledge again, with the warm water washing over me. The waterfall represented Tlazoteotl's cleansing force and my resurfacing from the water represented the rebirth of my health and innocence.

I used the Tlazoleotl posture frequently over the next several years and experienced her cleansing as ridding me of my cancerous cells. She has become one of the more important postures for me.

Susanne's cleansing by Tlazolteotl, her first experience with the goddess, occurred when she was blind as to the intent of the posture, yet its imagery made its intent crystal clear. This experience is noteworthy in that it also included aspects of the healing Bear as well.

4-14-08: Milk squirted out of my breasts into my hands and overflowed onto the ground, where it splashed up. Out of some of the upward splashes little beings with blue baseball caps, mostly like little bees but with human like faces, flew off. Then I felt very hollow and empty, as if the rhythm of the drumming was all I had inside my body. I morphed into a hollow tree trunk, where a woodpecker appeared intermittently. Then I saw a bear

Tlazolteotl Posture

Stand with your feet parallel and knees slightly bent. Your hands are held in front of your chest, as though you are cupping your breasts, with your fingers curled so that your fingernails face forward and point upward. Your face looks straight ahead, with your upper teeth extended over your lower lip, with your upper lip raised so that your teeth are visible. Your eyes are closed.

and followed it into a cave, where I snuggled up to it for a long winter's nap. Then I felt a light energy, kind of golden, coming into my hands, and I then was holding a rainbow.

Once Susanne was cleansed by the purging of the milk, she felt a significant loss of a part of herself but couldn't yet identify what that loss was. It left her temporarily feeling empty and hollow, like the hollow tree in her trance. This hollowness was briefly threatened by a woodpecker, but then she found warmth and closeness to the healing Bear, which brought her a new energy. At the time we did not discuss or need to discuss what was healed, though healing was apparent with her experience of light golden energy and a rainbow in her hands, leaving her feeling purified.

When I followed up by sharing this description with Susanne three years later, she reported: "I felt particularly healed by this experience, and it gave me a strong sense of spiritual connection. I thought this experience was also very appropriate to my profession as a psychotherapist, since people tell me of their pain—"filth"—and I help to facilitate it being transformed into something positive."

Susanne had not yet experienced the Bear Spirit posture, but the Bear Spirit is probably the most common spirit guide and so frequently appears spontaneously in a person's ecstatic experience. From my own experience as a psychotherapist who has on occasion carried with me the "filth" of a client, I suggested that if Susanne tends to take this "filth" on herself, she would feel very empty when cleansed of it, which may at first feel threatening, but with insight and the help of the nurturing spirit of the bear, she would feel free and would see a rainbow at the end.

THE HEALING COUPLE

The Couple of Cernavoda is done by a couple, male and female partners, working together to increase the healing energy of the female partner and thus her ability to heal those seeking her help.

In this posture the male and female positions are different, as depicted by the ancient figurines showing these postures that were found in a 7,000-year-old grave on the Danube River near Cernavoda, Romania. The male's posture in particular is quite common in many other places around the world. When these postures are used separately, the trance experiences are weak, but when a woman works with a male partner who sends her his energy, her healing energy is exponentially increased. Just as the male partner directs or focuses his energy to his female partner, the female partner directs her warmth and healing energy to the person who seeks her help. Her healing energy is greatly increased through the synergy of the couple working together.

In asking the question, "What do these postures kinesthetically express?" the male partner with his fists pressed into his cheeks shows great focus on some thought. From our experience with this posture, this thought is of focusing and directing energy to his female partner. The female partner with her head up is focusing her attention somewhere beyond herself, and with her fingers touching her knee in a tender manner she is expressing a feeling of tenderness, feelings of care and healing. She is sending outward energy to heal.

In the following example however, the healing energy was not sent outward but was used by the female partner to heal herself. As the male partner who sent my energy to my female partner, I did not feel a great depletion of my own energy. Since warmth provides healing, the Couple of Cernavoda is extremely effective because of the great increase in the healing energy of the female healer sent to her by her male counterpart, as shown in the example below. On one occasion in our weekly group I sat in the posture facing Virginia and sent her healing energy. My own experience with the posture found me in a yellow-golden bubble or aura; as I exhaled, the bubble would balloon out in front of me, and like a child blowing soap bubbles, a small bubble would break free and hit Virginia, disintegrating into smaller bubbles or spots as they hit and entered her. I envisioned these bubbles as bubbles of healing light energy being sent to Virginia, and

The Couple of Cernavoda Posture

female position

male position

In this posture the woman sits on the floor with the left leg firmly extended straight out in front of her body. Her left foot is flexed at a right angle. The right knee is raised, with the sole of the right foot resting flat on the floor beside the left knee. Both elbows are bent and pointing away from the body, and the fingers rest one on either side of the bent kneecap, palms down, thumbs close to the other fingers with fingers lightly touching her kneecap. The right hand is cupped with palm uplifted or raised off the knee, and the left hand is stiff with the wrist arched slightly downward. The spine is erect, with neck extended upward.

The man sits on a low stool or firm pillows. Feet are on the floor in front of the body pointing forward, about eight or ten inches part. The elbows rest on the knees. Lean forward slightly so that the jaw can rest on the upraised fisted hands. Allow the weight of the head to be supported by the fists so that the fists push the skin upward, making folds in the skin of your cheeks.

with them she experienced a greater sense of energy and well-being. Virginia reported:

> 2-26-08: I decided to experience this as a healing for my acoustic neuroma, with Nick's energy supplementing mine. I could feel something like an electric current on the left side of my face, running in the vicinity from the ear to eye and from the side of my face to the corner of my mouth. Quickly, I could feel my body heating up. It became very hot, almost enough to sweat. Then it cooled and never got really hot again, though it remained warm. For the rest of the time I simply tried to empty thoughts from my mind and feel this energy or whatever happened. It was intense and positive. The electric current like energy is gone now.

Virginia's feelings of warmth and healing were intensified by my energy being added to her own, increasing the force of her healing energy. Though we typically think of healers working by themselves in their practice, there can be a great benefit in working with a partner. As a psychologist I have had the occasional opportunity to work with a co-therapist and have always found greater energy in the therapy session. In the literature of shamanism there are occasional stories of husband and wife shaman working together. Having a partner in the healing arts is not always possible or feasible, but I believe that there can be a great benefit to the additional synergy it provides.

UZBEK SHAMANIC HEALER

This Chiltan Spirits posture has been found all around the world and one of the oldest examples of it was found in Bolivia from about 3,000 years ago. The myth of this posture told by a contemporary Uzbek sha-man who uses it seems to define the nature of the experience: in this trance the shaman is said to summon the spirits of forty-one female knights who assist him in his work of healing. When a healer calls upon the flow or transmission of warming energy to heal additional energy is beneficial, increasing the effectiveness whether it comes from the Bear Spirit, from a partner as in the Couple of Cernavoda, or from the spirits of forty-one female knights.

This posture has one version for a man and another for a woman. The shaman or shamaness using this posture frequently experiences multiple energies, originating from the forty-one female knights. So often in this posture one may feel crowded by all of these spirits. On one occasion I felt them circling around me, sending me great warmth. Because of the increased energy supplied by the knight spirits, the Chiltan Spirits can be used for healing others, even from a distance.

Sarah's ecstatic experiences continually amaze me with the fullness of their detailed imagery. Her first experience with the Chiltan Spirits, with its themes of abandonment, survival, and reunion, reminded me of a number of ancient healing myths of abandonment and then growth into extraordinary strength, such as in the story of Beowulf in Anglo-Saxon mythology and in The Cuchulain of Muirthemne, which is a retelling of the Cú Chulainn legends of Irish mythology.

3-3-08: I saw a huge tree twisting back and forth with great and growing energy, over and over until it twisted itself out of the ground and started walking about. It was joined by a large white bear. It looked like a polar bear. The bear caressed and rubbed against the tree in warm friendship, and they were walking through the woods together when they encountered a large basket of laundry covered with leaves. The bear pulled out a shirt and some socks, and the tree wanted to wear them, as well as some pants and towels and shirts, on its branches. After the tree donned all the clothing, at the bottom of the basket was a human baby. The tree wanted the bear to put the baby on one of its crotches, but the bear wanted to carry the baby. The tree wanted the baby badly and said it could ride in its hollow trunk, but there was a woodpecker that was not happy with all the moving around and did not want to share its space. So the bear carried

Chiltan Spirits Posture

(Left: male position; right: female position)

The Chiltan Spirits has a female version and a male version; the only difference between the two is that the shaman stands with feet apart, toes pointing forward, whereas the shamaness sits in an easy cross-legged position with her right leg folded in front of her left. In both postures, the left arm rests against the waist with the palm of the left hand just right of the navel, palm facing toward the body. The right arm angles up along the torso, with the right palm resting on the left breast. The upper arms rest against the side of the body.

the baby, and they all walked together for months, through many, many changing seasons, and the baby was rapidly growing and walking on its own. And then when the baby was about a teenager, the tree started to lose some of its branches and started to die. The group found themselves in the place where the bear and tree had found the baby. An old woman was there, looking for something. She told the bear she had left a basket of laundry there and had returned for it. They told her about the baby, and she hugged the teenage boy and the tree. The tree then re-rooted and grew all healthy and green again.

Here, healing energy was provided by Mother Earth in the form of her flora and fauna, the tree and bear—another appearance by the Bear Spirit—who together became foster parents, nurturing the baby until he became a teenage boy and was finally reunited with his mother. During medieval times in Europe, children were often fostered to the prominent and wealthier families of the community, who were better able to care for them than their own parents. As with Beowulf and Cuchulain, there are many such stories of uprooted, fostered youth growing to extraordinary strength. Though in this story the tree eventually began to die, once the boy was reunited with his mother and the tree re-rooted itself, the tree flourished again. This story was highly relevant to Sarah, as she herself was adopted, and had a number of unresolved issues concerning her relationship with her adopted parents, especially with her adopted father who had wanted a boy, which became an issue as she matured into womanhood. These issues will be explored in more depth later in this book.

When I shared my interpretation with Sarah, she saw it as being completely valid and complementary to her own interpretation. For her, the white bear in the trance was a healer. "For some reason, the old woman lost track of the boy hidden in the basket, perhaps causing this need for healing. I assume that because the boy matured, he was healed by the bear, but it took the old woman's return to heal the tree." The tree, she said, seemed to have a desire to be human. It gradually started to die perhaps from the exhaustion of watching the boy for so many years without being able to possess him. This would explain the tree's healing by the old woman when they returned her son to her. Sarah said the experience offered her a valuable life lesson: "Sometimes, it takes a long time to find out who we are because of ego and distractions. However, to be who we are meant to be is to be rooted. This is what the journey says to me. I remember that when I had this vision, the emphasis for me was strongly on the tree."

6
Divination Postures

Determining the Nature of Healing and the Outcome of Events

When we lack a deeper understanding of the nature of our old, dysfunctional beliefs and patterns, we may choose from any of the divination, spirit journeying, and metamorphosis postures to uncover the specific nature of a dysfunctional belief or problem. Such a combination of postures, done sequentially, can be a powerful method for effecting change and facilitating healing. In fact, drawing from the different categories of postures when addressing certain problems or issues can often be the best way to use ecstatic trance for self-healing. Sometimes the discovery of exactly what has been healed does not occur after one's first experience with a posture; it may take several experiences, spaced apart, and sometimes with different postures, to integrate the knowledge that has been revealed. This is why working sequentially with different categories of postures can work so well. Case in point is a healing experience I had that involved three different Mesoamerican deities: the Olmec Diviner, the Feathered Serpent, and Tlazolteotl—postures of divination, initiation, and healing, respectively.

Divination experiences, in particular, can open the door by answering questions concerning what is needed for healing and spiritual growth, and can be a good way to kick-start a sequence that leads to deeper healing. In addition, a divination posture can also point you in the right direction, as far as unspoken or unconscious concerns.

SACRIFICING TO FIND PEACE
IN A MAYAN VILLAGE

I will first introduce the Olmec Diviner.

The Olmec culture occurred in what is now present-day Mexico between 1100 and 500 BCE. A friend of Belinda Gore's found a picture of this figure among her mother's belonging after her death.[1] Other than it being typical of the Olmec culture, very little is known about it except that, through experiencing the posture and because of its physical similarity to other divination postures such as the Lady of Cholula and even the Jama Coaque Diviner, which we will see later in this chapter, the Olmec Diviner has been determined to be a divination posture. The variations in these postures offer us some flexibility for comfort, but each essentially expresses the same feeling of opening one up in curious and wondering thought to seek answers to questions, whether conscious or unconscious.

On 9-8-08 when I first experienced the ancient, thatched-hut Mayan village using the Olmec Diviner, I sensed that one of the village people was my wife, though I do not think I took to the diviner a specific question. This was our group's first experience with the diviner and the others in the group did not know its intent, though I did, because I read about the posture before selecting it. During that experience I was greeted by a priestess of the Feathered Serpent while at a nearby pyramid. She asked me to make a sacrifice of a piglet. I chose a female piglet, which was more valuable than a male, and while doing so I had the feeling that my wife, who was looking on when I chose the animal from our stock back at the village, appreciated what I was doing. During this experience, I was not precisely sure what of myself I was sacrificing, but I had a vague idea that it had something to do with my relationship with my wife.

Then, during an experience with Tlazolteotl, I returned to the same village, and the goddess showed me that this issue had been resolved, hence the feeling of peace I experienced.

Olmec Diviner Posture

Sit on the floor. Your left leg rests on the floor out to the side with knee bent, with the upper part of the leg at a 45-degree angle from your body and the lower leg (below the knee) turned inward toward the midline of the body. Your right leg is bent and off the floor with knee raised, such that you can rest the inner side of your elbow on the knee, with your forearm hanging down in front of your leg. Relax your hand with your fingers slightly curled. The bottom of your left foot rests against the side of your right foot. Cup your left hand and rest it on the inside of your leg, above the knee. Hold your arm rigid and slightly away from your body. Your head faces straight ahead; your eyes are closed, and your mouth is slightly open.

4-18-10: I was at the Mayan temple just sitting on one of the lower steps when a woman in a white robe, carrying a brass bowl, came and sat next to me, a priestess of Tlazolteotl. I said to her that my mind has been racing with too much going on. She said nothing but just looked at me and I felt a peacefulness. Eventually she looked to my left, her right, at the small settlement nearby of several, 3 to 4 grass huts. I looked too and felt the peacefulness of the people—a child rolling a hoop, a woman in front of one hut weaving and another grinding corn—very peaceful with the people doing what was expected of them. I had been to this place before, then one of them was my wife, but now I was by myself as if arriving there from the future.

The issue that was healed with my sacrifice had to do with an issue of having to sacrifice my attempts to control some things about my wife. I often use the dreamwork technique of taking an element from an experience such as the sacrifice in the earlier experience and ask, "What part of me am I sacrificing?" With that question the answer came to me, "My attempts to control."

At the time I thought the second experience at the same village had resolved the issue for me. However, some time later, I had two more experiences related to this same issue, which put me in contact with two of my power animals, an eagle and a coyote. This entire sequence brought me to a new level of freedom in my life, freedom from what was eating at me in the form of cancer, and a higher level of self-actualization, as I was able to resolve my role in a long-standing relationship issue, as described in chapter 9. This shows the important role of divination postures in determining our problems and launching us on a path of self-exploration and healing; in this case, the Olmec Diviner knew my problem even before I was fully aware of it, showing me something important about my relationship with my wife, and setting me on a course of discovery.

Finding answers to one's questions is one of the main reasons for using a divination posture. There are basically two types of divination experiences: those in which we find answers to questions, spoken and unspoken, that arise from one's unconscious mind, and those that connect us with universal mind, which can be used to predict future events and trends. In either case, asking questions of a divination posture may be the best way to determine the nature of the healing that is required. Be forewarned that the answer to a question may be somewhat cryptic when it comes through imagery or metaphor. That is why wording of the question is important, because the more specific and exact we can be, the more concrete the answer. Answers may at times be very uncompromising, and not something one may want to hear. Sometimes the truth hurts!

THE WISE OLD GRANDMOTHER

The statuette of Lady of Cholula was found in Cholula, an important indigenous religious center in the Puebla province of central Mexico and the site of a huge archeological complex dominated by the Great Pyramid of Cholula, called Tlachihualtepetl (Nahuatl for "artificial mountain"). It was established by the Toltecs and later became an Aztec city devoted to the worship of Quetzalcoatl, the Feathered Serpent. The statuette is pre-Columbian, dating from around 1350 CE. The Lady of Cholula is a wise old grandmother who can lovingly set things straight for you and, if necessary, be sufficiently blunt to keep you from wallowing in problems that have become comfortable little ruts. If the truth is your goal, the Lady will help you get to it by the most direct route.

The clay figure of this posture shows the Lady wearing a hat and a collar. The hat is cone-shaped and pointed, with "fingers" radiating from the base. The collar is circular, extending over her shoulders, chest, and back. These props, should you choose to create them for yourself, may heighten or intensify your trance.[2]

I usually do not ask people in our group to tell the group the question they asked the Lady of Cholula because I want them to feel free to ask the most personal questions. Such was the case for Virginia.

Lady of Cholula Posture

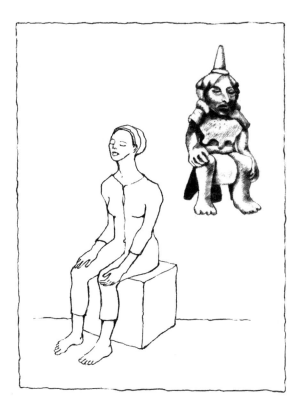

Sit in a chair with your legs apart and your feet pointed straight ahead. Cup your left hand around the front of your left knee. Rest your right hand palm-down with the fingers forward on your right leg, just above the knee and slightly to the right. Your left arm should be somewhat tensed as it is pulled forward, while your right arm is more relaxed. Depending on the height of the chair and the length of your legs, it may be necessary to put a cushion under your feet to raise them so you can clasp your knee. Lean forward slightly, with your spine straight, hinging forward from the hips. Hold your head straight with your eyes closed but looking forward under your eyelids. Your tongue should protrude gently from between your lips.

2-26-08: I am walking through a jungle with a tiger on my right. All I see is the green of the jungle. Immediately around us the terrain morphs into an African plain. We come to a pond with light coming down from the sky. I ask for an angel or something like that to appear. Then the good witch of The Wizard of Oz appears. She says the tiger, which is also me, has to change its stripes. Colors flash through my mind, but none seem acceptable. The tiger shrinks into a ball and then rolls into the water. I follow, and we swim like dolphins for a while, then emerge on the land, where the tiger slowly splits into two forms, a tiger and a hawk. In the end the tiger walks on the ground, no longer in a jungle, while the hawk sits high in a tree.

Though I did not know Virginia's question, if this had been my experience I might ask, "What about me needs to change colors?" I might also ask, "What are the characteristics of a tiger, a dolphin, and a hawk?" Another pertinent question to ask would be, "What part of me is the tiger that needs to split into a hawk?" Initially in the experience, Virginia rejects the suggestion that she needs to change colors, as shown by her assessment that none of the colors are "acceptable." However, she may find the answer to what aspect of herself or life needs to change colors has something to do metaphorically with emerging on the land and splitting.

In the following experience, the message I received from the Lady of Cholula was that she would not answer my question. I was looking at the water where I was expecting to see an image, an answer to my unspecified question, but the Lady of Cholula showed me that she would not answer my question. I think maybe she thought my question was meaningless chatter, like the image of the muskrat that appeared in the trance, chattering away meaninglessly—an example of the Lady's sense of humor. Most likely I was asking a question to which I already knew the answer but was hoping for a different response.

1-27-09: I'm on the edge of a tarn that is spring fed above our place. I'm looking into the water—the ripples prevent me from seeing an image. The colors, oranges and reds are there but broken up. Then a muskrat crawls out, next to an altar/sacred structure opposite me. I crawl around the tarn to my left and come close to the muskrat who is chattering at me. I wonder what he is trying to tell me. Then I slid into the pool and go down to his hole and crawl in. It opens up into quite a spacious place. I lay there. He comes in still chattering to me in an agitated manner.

Though Maria later reported that she entered the Lady posture with no specific thoughts or concerns in the following experience, I do know that she had just found a snakeskin in her front yard—and she had an extreme aversion to snakes. I had the opportunity to visit Maria a couple of years later at her father's remote mountain retreat center, where she stood showing no fear while we watched a snake climbing in a stand of bamboo, so obviously she benefitted from her experience with the Lady.

11-19-07: I opened my eyes (not actually) and began to move forward. I was moving like a snake, snug to the ground. I resisted this for a long while because of my aversion to snakes and my fears, but I eventually gave in. After some time I moved slowly forward again. This time I was shedding my skin. I felt so vibrant, changed—awake and new. A voice chanted for a long time the words "I am." If I become the feared snake, how can I still be afraid?

As I thought about this ecstatic experience three years later, I e-mailed Maria, asking her to tell me more about this experience. She reported that the most powerful part was the feeling of opening her eyes for the first time. "This snake experience was powerful to me in that I was actually overcoming fear rather than just processing it.

The feeling of opening my eyes for the first time was so new, because it was the first time I was a snake, seeing the world through snake eyes. I couldn't be afraid of myself, so in the end there was nothing to fear." That's the essence of the Lady of Cholula: direct and uncompromising.

THE ECUADORIAN DIVINER

Like the similarly named Jama-Coaque Metamorphosis posture, which is introduced in chapter 8, the Jama-Coaque Diviner figurine was found on the northern coast of Ecuador, at Jama, which was a market center for the Jama-Coaque culture, one of the planet's oldest and most advanced. The Jama-Coaque people thrived thousands of years ago and were known for their maritime skill as well as skill in various art forms, including pottery, as evidenced primarily by the manufacture of strikingly realistic human figures in clay, such as this one. No doubt their shamanic skills were as great as their arts.

The intent of virtually all the postures has been revealed by either Felicitas Goodman or Belinda Gore, except in the case of this Jama-Coaque Diviner. I found this figurine in the Quai Branly Museum in Paris, which features the indigenous art, cultures, and civilizations of Africa, Asia, Oceania, and the Americas. I was fascinated by it—a posture different from the Jama-Coaque Metamorphosis figure, but still of the Jama-Coaque culture, no doubt about it. I decided to pursue uncovering the intent of this posture for myself and tried it with two different groups: the nine people in the group who met regularly in my home, and a group of twenty-four people who were attending the 2009 International Association for the Study of Dreams conference. In addition, at my request, Belinda Gore used this posture in one of her groups and came to the same conclusion that I had: that it is indeed a divination posture.

In these groups we entered the posture with the question, "What do you have to show me, tell me, or take me to?" I expected this question

Jama-Coaque Diviner Posture

Sit on the floor with your knees pulled up in front of you such that your feet are flat on the floor or ground, and when you lean forward with a straight back, hinging from the hips, you can comfortably rest your right forearm across your raised knees. The elbow of your right arm is on your right knee and the hand of your right arm is resting on your left knee. Your knees and feet should be about ten inches apart. The elbow of your left arm rests on the back of your right hand. Your left hand is raised, palm toward your face, with the fingers together in a loose fist. Your head is tilted slightly upward and facing forward.

would reveal the intent of the posture, but now I realize that for a diviner such as Jama-Coaque, the question assumes that he already knows the unspoken concern or problem that we bring to him, and he therefore provides the answer to that concern. One person, who experienced this posture at the IASD conference, said her trance addressed a concern in her life that she later revealed to me: she had been entertaining a fantasy for several years, about moving away from Rio to a small village.

> *6-30-09: I saw myself packing my stuff, thinking of where to put it and wondering whether I would be living with some friends or renting a place of my own, and then wondering how it would be different if I moved to another country. A major concern was whether or not I would have sufficient income given that I am currently living off of my savings, but at the same time I felt certain that money would not be a big problem. I was aware of the tension in my body and still was able to stay still. I even enjoyed the discomfort of the position and my being able to hold it, though I changed my posture quite often, for my legs and arms tend to become numb when I don't move.*

It seems that Jama-Coaque supported her thoughts of moving away from Rio, given her positive feelings in holding the posture and her intuitive interpretation of Jama-Coaque's response to her unvoiced question. In talking with her after the workshop she seemed committed to moving, though I do not know if she did.

Again, using the Jama-Coaque Diviner posture without knowing its intent or without any specific question of the posture other than "What do you have to show me, tell me, or take me to?" Cynthia, from the IASD conference, had the following ecstatic trance experience.

> *6-30-09: A leopard or jaguar—a spotted panther—came up to me and invited me to follow it, which I did. I soon realized it would be easier to*

walk through the jungle on all fours, which I did. We came to a tree, which we circled a few times, then jumped up into it. It showed me how to lie across a branch, paws dangling to relieve my back pain. I took this position (I was a cat too now and had been since I got on all fours). By the way, I really enjoyed being a jungle cat.

When I contacted Cynthia eighteen months later, she told me she had interpreted this experience as offering an antidote for an arthritic condition that had developed only recently. "I have to say that if I could find a way to get into this posture—suspended prone with limbs hanging relaxed—I would! It seems like it would gently relieve many joints, neck, shoulders, hips, etc., of the pressure of bearing weight and let them stretch naturally with gravity. This was not a problem at the time, but this summer I ended up hobbling around on a knee that stayed painful for weeks. . . . Maybe I was also being encouraged to 'hang in there.'" This experience is one example of how future concerns or problems can be addressed through a divination posture such as Jama-Coaque, who can give us solutions before we even know the problem.

I was able to contact Tom eighteen months after the IASD conference, and upon learning that this particular Jama-Coaque posture is a divination posture, he was able to "connect the dots" concerning the ecstatic experience he had with the Jama-Coaque Diviner—an experience that was not only a teaching, but a foretelling.

6-30-09: I am being carried as a king (perhaps wounded?), but in a victory celebration. Am I to be sacrificed by this group of African tribesmen? Around us the village celebrates. Upon arriving at the foot of a volcano I am helped down. A white horse comes to me, kneeling in humility, and lets me mount. I ride back and forth in front of the gathered people. Everyone cheers and I wave. Then I dismount and slap the white horse on the rump and it goes back from whence it came. A donkey is then brought forward and I mount it as a symbol of the humility with which I want to lead the people. Then I get off and walk through the crowd. I put children [in turns] on the burro's back, helping them on and off, giving them rides. Then my body shifts with the rhythm of the drum and I become the rhythm of the drum. My body is shaking during this portion of the meditation with the beat of the drum. The drum starts spinning around my heart, healing, and then I call for my white horse, and on it I circle the gathered village people, blessing them. Finally, I fly off the horse and arrive at my home in North Carolina, able to bring it to order.

It turned out Tom had been planning an important conference that was to take place about four months after his trance experience with Jama-Coaque, and this was the main concern on his mind at the time. This was to be his fifth annual conference, he had organized the four previous conferences successfully, thus in his trance he arrives on the scene as a king being carried by the people. In reality, Tom finds planning these conferences very anxiety provoking, as he has to sacrifice about half of his time to do the work. He recognized within his experience that he might be sacrificed to the volcano, so his anxiety over planning the event might have to be sacrificed. Yet his strength and confidence was validated by the appearance of the white horse coming to him. He willingly and humbly sacrificed himself to plan the conference, as seen in his move from the white horse to the burro. In planning such conferences, Tom values what he expects the attendees—the children in his trance—will learn and how they will benefit; this he has to offer the world and future generations. Planning the conference required from him a full measure of his servant-leadership energy, but at its closing ceremony, the participants were enthusiastic and grateful—the image of blessing the cheering people before riding off. Through this experience, Tom received a future vision of the courage he will summon despite his anxiety, and his success as a result. Jama-Coaque responds to his unspoken concern unequivocally: he will return home as a king, on the back of his white horse, realizing that the real power of the king is in being the humble servant.

Two other divination postures, the Nupe Mallam Diviner and the Mayan Oracle, described in chapter 9, illustrate another function of divination postures: that of helping us attain a greater degree of self-actualization.

7

Initiation Postures

Dying to Old Patterns, Rebirthing a New Self

Initiation or death-rebirth experiences embody the cycles of life, from birth and maturity to decay and death, a process that then leads to rebirth, the spring of life. These experiences reveal the death of some aspect of the person that may be considered a fault or immaturity, or the death of a pattern of thinking or a belief that was adopted early in life as a survival strategy but that no longer works for the evolved person. Initiation postures can offer a type of deep healing, helping us die to these kinds of old beliefs and mental patterns we have subconsciously adopted, so that we can become reborn to a new, healthier, authentic self.

Following the Cuyamungue Method of working with postures, group discussion after the ecstatic trance experience generally examines how a person's experiences matches what is believed to be the intent of the posture, and does not always focus on how the experience may have changed the individual, in the case of the initiation postures what of the person died and what was reborn. The method recognizes that this change happens though it is often not conscious. Yet, as a psychologist, and for the purpose of this book, I have been interested in investigating the change brought about by the ecstatic experience whenever possible.

THE DEITY OF CREATION AND LIGHT

The Feathered Serpent, the Toltec deity Quetzalcoatl (600 BCE to 900 CE), the source of the breath of life and fertility, takes us through the cycle of death and rebirth. The magical appearance of Quetzalcoatl (in the Mayan culture, Kukulcán) on the pyramidal structure at Chichén Itzá, in the Yucatan, each year at the spring and fall equinox is a significant cultural event that signals a renewal of life for Mesoamerica. Though Quetzalcoatl's images are ubiquitous throughout Mesoamerica, this posture is found in its essential form in all areas of the world. For example, Heidimarie Graf, a practitioner of ecstatic posture work from Austria, sent me a picture of a male figure from Denmark in the same posture, which I have used to the same effect; there this figure is called the Nyborg Man.

Most ecstatic experiences of initiation, in which there is death and rebirth, begin with negative, sinister, or painful images, and end with a positive and pleasant experience—a rebirth. In this sense, initiation experiences are healing. Take, for example, Virginia's experience of 11-5-07 with the Feathered Serpent. She reported that her journey started out with muted or subtle images. Then, about a third of the way into the experience, she saw two figures shrouded in a murky light. "The scene was of a shorter female person of indeterminate age reaching up to the taller, shadowy figure in front of her. The taller figure was still, almost like a statue, a dark shadow. The shorter person, whose back was toward me, started pulling off mud cakes, mud, or hard dirt from the head of the taller person. Underneath was a dark, stern face; when that pulled away, a softer face; then a much softer face, until it was like the face of the Virgin, looking down and to the right."

Virginia's experience started out murky and shadowy; there was an uneasy feeling, with one figure clawing at another, pulling off mud; with each layer removed, the figure became softer, until finally the face of the Madonna emerged, conveying a sense of love. The transformation from the figure caked with mud to the soft face of Madonna indicates

Feathered Serpent Posture

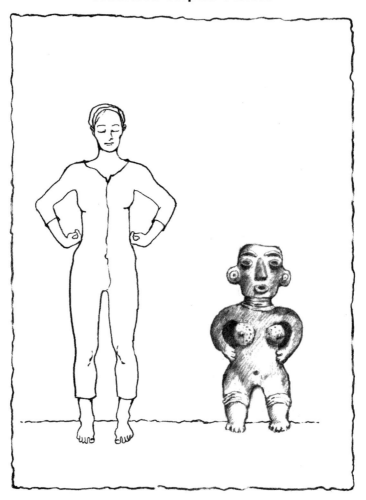

Stand with your feet parallel, about six inches apart, knees lightly bent with toes pointing straight forward. Cup your hands and place them at your side at waist level, with fingers curling upward and your arms rounded outward with bent elbows pointing to either side. Your face looks straight ahead, and your eyes are closed and your mouth slightly open.

that a healing or rebirth, whether physical or emotional, took place. How she more specifically changed was not indicated, though I expect that it brought her to a new feeling or sense of compassion.

According to Belinda Gore, the intent of the initiation experience of the Feathered Serpent Posture is first to enter "a womblike place, perhaps a cave or a warm, dark environment. After resting there for a while, you then rise to a new life."[1] In her trance, Janice saw a bear scratching a tree, felt its warm and cozy fur, and then became the bear. Seeing snow fall, she entered a cave, rolled into a ball, and fell into a deep sleep, "to hibernate and incubate." Then, she rolled over, awakened, and stepped out of the cave with two baby cubs to be greeted by springtime. She saw an elk stag running with a herd and joined them, running freely, to a big waterfall where all the animals gathered. This experience illustrates the death-rebirth cycle, in which she entered the cave to die to her old self, and came out in the springtime rested and running free.

Afterward Janice talked some about having to leave her husband and live alone for a while. Though the home she would be leaving felt warm and cozy, womblike just as in her trance experience, she needed to go through the cold of winter to find a new life, which in the end might provide new friendships or relationships, like those at the waterfall where the animals gathered.

THE CYCLE OF LIFE

The naked figure of the Lady of Thessaly, who has a bird face, was found in the area of Thessaly, Greece, and dates from around 6000 BCE. Belinda Gore says that during this Neolithic period, "the feminine principle was related to the sun and women took the form of birds."[2] With this posture the feminine principle is witnessed in the cycle of life and the creation of Earth, experiencing the woman's womb as the continually renewing source of that creation with concern for the Earth and environment through the birth of each morning and the rising sun. While the Feathered Serpent posture is concerned with the death and rebirth of personal issues, the Lady of Thessaly is concerned more with the unity of the cycle of life rather than representing specific experiences of death and rebirth. In comparing the two postures as to the feelings they express, the Feathered Serpent exudes the feeling of defiance, the feeling of "I am ready to face the pain of death and rebirth with strength," whereas the Lady of Thessaly is more nurturing, feminine, and voluptuous—the source of life and rebirth. Depending upon the attitude or feeling behind how a person is facing a particular issue in their life, I would suggest the person use the posture that best reflects that emotion or need.

Belinda Gore reports that this posture is traditionally used by women. Being so informed, I naturally wanted to see what would happen if I used it, and my first experience with this posture seemed quite significant for me as a man.

7-16-09: At first I found myself sitting on a rock at the edge of the water in Greece, but then the setting switched to Copenhagen, and the famous statue of the Little Mermaid there. Seagulls were flying around and landing around me, and dolphins broke the surface of the water. A gull landed on my shoulder and the weight was just enough to push me into the water, where I swam freely. Then I came to Poseidon holding his trident and seated on his throne, and I didn't want it to be him, so the image switched to that of Njord, the Norse god of the sea, wind, and fertility. He told me to enjoy the weightlessness of moving through the water, then sent me on to his mother, who smiled warmly as I approached her and told me I am doing a good job.

The elements of this more feminine posture emerged with my initial rejection of the Greek god, Poseidon, a more masculine warrior-like god, and my seeking of the Nordic god, Njord, who is of the clan of fertility gods and goddesses, though both Poseidon and Njord are gods of the sea. Njord then sends me to the Great Mother, who accepts me with warmth and encouragement, allowing me to acknowledge my own

Lady of Thessaly Posture

Sit on the floor with your knees bent and both legs folded toward your right. The weight of your body is primarily on your left but-tock. Your feet should be relaxed, with no effort made to point your toes. Tuck your left foot under your right knee. Hold your left arm rigid, with your left hand palm down on your left knee, fingers pointing toward a spot about one foot in front of the middle of your body. Your right arm is more relaxed, with your right hand resting over your right knee, fingers pointing toward the same midpoint, slightly in front of the midpoint of the body. Elongate your neck and turn your head so that you are looking over your right knee.

feminine side. Njord, being a fertility god, was more nurturing and offered support for my feminine side, while staying with Poseidon would likely have stimulated my more aggressive and masculine side. If I had used the Feathered Serpent posture, I might have stayed with Poseidon. Afterwards I felt very nurtured and positive about the support this experience provided for the rebirth of my feminine aspects, something I apparently needed as I was led to seek Njord rather than Poseidon. Even though Gore has used this posture only with women, I feel that there is a real benefit in using it with men and hope to eventually use this posture with other men to see how they experience it.

Gerry's journey with the Lady of Thessaly was more typical of a woman's experience with this initiation posture.

8-16-09: A small band of nearly naked women, men, and children, wearing head wreathes and carrying baskets, walks to the beach beside the sea. An island is seen in the distance. I am one of five priestesses who make boats of leaves, filling them with fruit, vegetables, and flowers to send to the island's goddess. Everyone sings and claps to honor the Great Goddess. The leaf boats set sail with fruit, vegetables and flowers, and the head wreaths become very beautiful with flowers. A fire is built, and singing, clapping, and dancing begin. After the dancing, a meal is eaten. Everyone participates in preparing and consuming the feast. As the sun sinks, the children are prepared for a quest. They must return home from the beach, even though this place is strange to them. The adults leave the children on the beach and go into the hills. Dolphins try to lead the children to the island, but the children resist. Overhead can be seen a flying bison and a rainbow-colored flying serpent. Flocks of small birds will eventually guide the children back home from the beach. The hills open up as caverns that connect and run through the hills. Lights on the walls predict the future of the children. The adults skate through the caverns on water skates until they come to the stairs to the town. Some will watch over the children so they come to no harm.

Gerry's experience was clearly an initiation experience in the classical sense, a rite of passage from childhood to young adulthood. She experienced the personal growth of becoming a priestess, of leading women in celebrating the Great Goddess and leading the young through a rite of passage toward greater independence and maturity, renewing the process of creation in which the death and rebirth experiene within the rite of passage is a dominant theme. This process appears to be a developing role in Gerry's struggle with life in terms of her role as a leader and healer in the community, a process that she is experiencing in a nurturing and feminine manner without the sense of defiance and aggressiveness that might have been experienced with the Feathered Serpent posture.

8
Spirit Journeying and Metamorphosis Postures
Finding New Perspectives

The spirit journeying postures take us to the three worlds: the Sky World, the Middle World or earthly realm, and the underworld or Lower World. There are also postures that take us to the Realm of the Dead. Our spirit guides can lead us on journeys to realms where our dysfunctional beliefs are revealed, along with a new way of being. Experiencing animals through shape-shifting, a form a metamorphosis, provides us with animal spirit guidance that can show us ways in which we can experience ourselves in a different form, thus giving us a new perspective on life.

What we can learn from such ecstatic experiences can change our lives, even if we don't completely understand the message of the experience, which is often the case. Such change can happen gradually over the course of several different postures. For example, a journey into the spirit world can uncover some issue that is causing a problem that a subsequent death-rebirth or healing posture experience can resolve. Such sequencing of postures can be powerful in effecting change, as we will discover in chapter 9, on attaining self-actualization.

JOURNEYING TO SKY WORLD TO
FIND ONE'S PURPOSE

The model for the oldest of the spirit journeying shamanic postures, the Venus of Galgenberg, was discovered in 1988 along the banks of the Danube River, near Krems, Austria. This tiny figurine measures only two-and-three-quarter inches tall and is about 32,000 years old. It is her upraised arm, at an angle of thirty-seven degrees, that provides us with a clue that this is a spirit journeying gesture toward the Sky World.*

Why undertake such a journey? Gore says we go to the Sky World "to find the patterns that are the original intention for the Earth. We can draw the energy of those patterns down to the Earth, to help bring ourselves, the Earth, and all the other children of the Earth into better alignment with these patterns . . . to help bring back the balance."[1] From the beginning of time, these patterns have been stored in energy fields or matrices that form the universal mind. In my experience with journeying to the Sky World, I believe that postures like the Venus of Galgenberg facilitate access to the universal mind, the universal higher consciousness or source of being, which can offer knowledge that can benefit oneself and one's family, tribe, community, and the planet.

In using this posture with a group of attendees at the 2010 conference of the International Association for the Study of Dreams, all of whom were experienced in dream work yet did not know the purpose of the posture, its intent was validated by many, including Sheila.

---

*This angle is significant because of two other very old spirit-journey postures for journeying to the Sky World, the 16,000-year-old Lascaux Cave posture, and the 4,000-year-old Osiris posture, which both recline at a slope of 37 degrees, with the feet lower than the head. To implement these postures, Goodman made wooden platforms sloping at the same angle, which have been dubbed "launching pads."

Venus of Galgenberg Sky World Posture

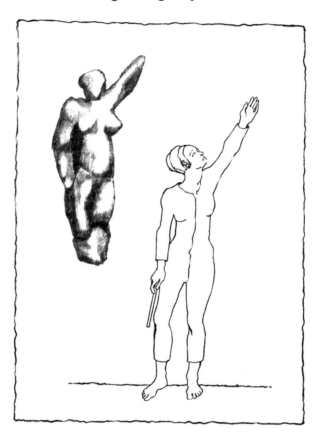

Stand with your left leg straight and your left foot pointing forward. Bend your right knee slightly, with your right foot slightly turned out, away from your body. The fingers of your right hand are together and point toward the ground, possibly holding a stick that rests along your right leg. Your left arm is raised at a 37-degree angle from the vertical line extending above your head, and that hand is cupped, with the palm of that hand turned toward that vertical line above your head. Your head is raised and turned toward the left, as though your eyes gaze at your raised hand, though your eyes remain closed.

6-28-10: My experience was of being in the forest. I was a native and was first placed by a fire to become purified. At some point I began to run through the forest with a cobra at my side. Then he hooded over me and we became one. We reached a cliff, went to jump, and at that point I changed into an eagle. Flying higher and higher, I merged with the sky and then with the sun. I was free and was one with the Creator's love. Being one with the Creator reminded me of the purpose of my life. I needed to return and went back to the fire. My attention was directed to my heart. It was at this time that I moved my extended hand to my heart. I remained in this posture for a minute or so and then returned to the posture. I remained at the fire to become purified to prepare my vehicle (body) for the golden light of creation.

This ecstatic experience typifies the intent of the Venus of Galgenberg; journeying to the Sky World—in this case, the sky and the sun—Sheila found the Creator's love, reminding her of her purpose in life, to show compassion to all those around her and to the Earth. This love energy is then drawn down to the earth on which Sheila stands, where she is purified by the fire and her body prepared to receive the golden light of Creation.

JOURNEYING TO THE MIDDLE WORLD

When journeying in the Middle World, we are taken to places we know on the surface of the Earth and to places frequented during our life, in a sense giving a review of our life before we journey beyond at the time of death. But before our death, while we still have time to experience life and grow, we have a lot to learn from remembering the places and events of our life—sometimes the painful memories that we have forgotten that need to be healed, sometimes the successes when we have forgotten what it takes for us to succeed.

In addition to taking me to known places the Middle World posture, the Priestess of Malta, has also taken me to other places around the world, places I have never been such as Eastern Peru, as described in chapter 2. It has also taken me to the places of my ancestors, from Germany and England, to New York, Pennsylvania, Ohio, and California. There is so much to learn in life, even from places we have never been and from our distant past.

The Priestess of Malta figurine dates from around 5,000 years ago. It was found on the island of Malta, in the Hypogeum, an underground labyrinth of chambers laboriously carved out of limestone with flint and obsidian tools some 5,000 years ago. Resembling the interior of a mega-lithic temple, the Hypogeum covers an area of more than 500 square meters, and descends three stories to a burial ground. The bones of over 7,000 people were found here. Evidence suggests that the Hypogeum was more than a giant mausoleum—it may also have been a place of worship and a training ground for the priestesses of Malta, which was a matri-archal society. The Priestess takes travelers on a spirit journey, typically flying or soaring across Earth, often touching down in one's daily envi-ronment but also in other places where we have something to learn.

My own experiences using the Priestess of Malta posture demon-strate how repeated trance work with the same posture can help to intensify a person's experience of the posture's intent. From my earliest journey to Peru, through a number of other Middle World journeys, to my very vivid ecstatic experience in January of 2011 where I found myself on a journey home to Denmark, I gained the belief that with the help of the Priestess of Malta I was able to communicate with and become my own ancestors.

1-6-11: I found myself leaving from the boat dock on a river in Nor-mandy. I was going up the coast and into the North Sea, around Jutland and down the east side toward what is now Germany. It is the beginning of winter and I am just getting home from my merchant trip. My first concern is of whether there are sufficient supplies for the family for winter. Did my sons and daughter do enough in preparation? My oldest son was left in charge. My wife was pregnant and doing little. She is almost due

Priestess of Malta Middle World Posture

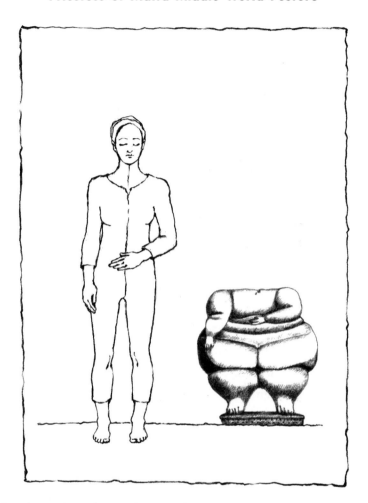

Stand straight with your feet parallel and slightly apart, toes pointed straight ahead and knees slightly bent. Your right arm is held firmly beside your body, locked at the elbow, with fingers hanging down. The palm of your left hand, with fingers and thumb together, rests against your waist with fingers over your navel. The elbow of your left arm is bent at 90 degrees and held close to your body. Face is forward, with eyes closed.

and my oldest daughter is with her, staying close to her. The year is maybe in the early 800s, several generations before the last experience I had in Normandy using the Hallstatt Warrior posture.

This was the beginning of about forty ecstatic experiences that opened the door to some incredible experiences, uncovering parts of my distant heritage in Scandinavia, some of these taking me back to the time when we worshipped the great mother goddess. These experiences have brought me to the realization of what the new world, the new age, now opening to us will be like and to the latest topic of writing and research I am pursuing.

JOURNEYING TO THE LOWER WORLD

In journeying into the Lower World we find ourselves underground in caves or under the sea where we often meet spirits—spirit guides in some cases and the spirits of the dead in others, spirits that have something to teach us or have the capability to heal us. Sometimes we uncover lost or unconscious memories. In this world I have met my spirit guide, the bear, but also a group of four men who I eventually realized were my spirits from the four directions, the first experience I present below. Each experience had something to teach me. I have also become different burrowing animals, a groundhog and mouse, which have taught me to nurture, to be patient, and to make myself heard.

One of the most effective postures for traveling to the Lower World is the Sami, by which one may enter the Lower World by moving down through such openings as whirlpools, tunnels, or spirals. These kinds of openings may be found in a cave, or sometimes through the bottom of the ocean—the typical motifs of this posture. This posture was found as an illustration in a seventeenth-century book, published in 1673 in Germany by J. Scheffer,[2] and includes a person drumming along with the person reclined in the underworld posture. The Sami are a tribe of reindeer herders from Lapland, Finland.

Sami Lower World Posture

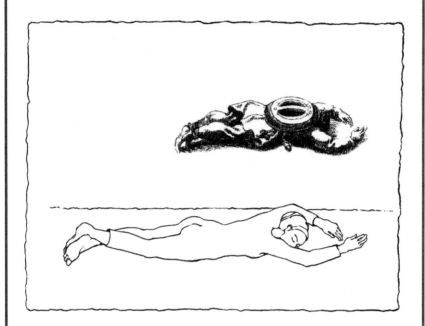

Lie on the floor on your stomach with your face down and arms extended above your head, with your right arm extended a little farther than your left. Rest your cupped hands with fingers together palm down on the floor about five inches apart. Extend your legs, with your right ankle crossed on top of your left ankle. Turn your head to the right.

Among the many possibilities for entering the Lower World, mine was through an abandoned railroad tunnel that had a downward entrance into a cave; what I found there was unexpected and extraordinary.

11-26-07: I went into the cave and found four men sitting in a circle around a fire. All were wearing bearskins. I joined them. I might have been wearing a bearskin, too. I listened to them, trying to understand what was

*going on. I was not sure. At first they seemed to be talking about a hunt,
then hunting for their enemy. When I finally understood, they were talking
about how they saw the world differently from other men, and somehow
they had found one another and could relate to one another with this
difference. They were sitting cross-legged, with their hands on their knees
in sort of a divination posture. They had found one another through the
experience of this posture. I realized I was one of them by finding them in
a similar manner. There was a bond between us.*

Again this experience was very early in my ecstatic experiences
and I did not go to this Sami warrior with any particular question.
The experience did validate the intent of the posture since I went
underground into a cave. Over the next several years I met these four
men in the cave on a number of occasions and eventually realized that
they are my spirit guides from the four directions. What this experience told me is that I could meet with others as they too journey into
the ecstatic world using the ecstatic postures, making the experience
quite extraordinary.

ENTERING THE REALM OF THE DEAD

One of the most fascinating spirit journeys one can undertake is to
the Realm of the Dead. In this world I have met with long dead ancestors, gone to Niflheim, the realm of those who died of illness and old
age from Nordic mythology, and on several occasions to a cave where
a group of spirits circling me, throwing sparks at me that entered my
body to destroy cancer cells. On one occasion I did not go underground
but was on a desolate hilltop at night again being circled by these spirits. The Realm of the Dead is a place where we meet spirits that heal or
teach us something.

Gore describes the typical trance experience of the traveler in such
a posture as wandering in a desolate area before coming to a deep pit in
which various spirits are encountered. "Often the person describes hav-

ing skin and muscle torn off until he or she is only bones. Eventually something changes, and the journeyer begins to rise into a new form and a new life,"[3] thus it can take the form of a death-rebirth experience. This posture is often used to reclaim a part of our soul or self that we have lost. Like all the spirit journeying postures, it is quite effective when used in combination with any of the other postures, in a sequence, to address an issue or concern.

The Hallstatt Warrior does not always take me into the Lower World, but I have found that I almost always meet some spirit guide or spirits of the dead, and as we will see, these spirits have something to teach me for my own personal healing or growth. It is this Realm of the Dead posture I use most frequently. This figure was found in Hirschlanden, Germany, the land of my ancestors, and dates from the fifth century BCE. I find the Hallstatt Warrior one of the most powerful postures for me because I feel considerable energy while holding my arms in this position and because it is such an archetypal male posture.

Journeying to the Realm of the Dead with the Hallstatt Warrior is a powerful avenue to opening a door to material that may have been forgotten or repressed, thus the experiences may be recognized as journeys into the unconscious mind. Because the ecstatic experience is in the language of metaphor, conscious understanding may be limited, but the unconscious mind understands this language and conscious understanding is not necessary. I have found that using hypnosis for this same purpose—that of going into the unconscious mind—requires the direction of verbal hypnotic suggestions from another person; the value of the ecstatic journey is that we can use the energy of the postures to directly gain direction and power.

Sarah's journey with the Hallstatt Warrior contains the hallmark features of traveling to the Realm of the Dead with the disintegration of her body that is then rebuilt with a strong backbone. With a white dove landing on her right shoulder and a mourning dove on her left, it is a clear death-rebirth experience so often expected when journeying

Hallstatt Warrior Spirit World Posture

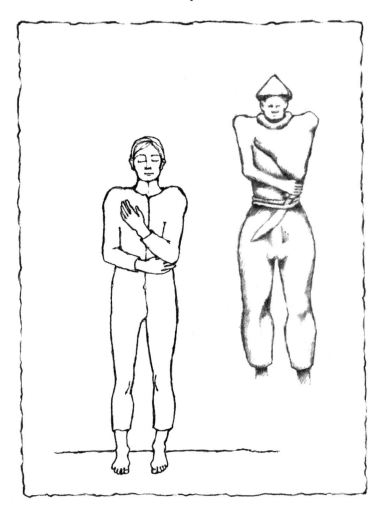

Stand with your feet about five inches apart and toes pointed forward. Keep your knees locked. Place your right arm along your waist, with the ball of your hand covering your navel. Your left arm rests along the side of your torso, with the left hand resting on the right breast, fingers pointing toward the right shoulder. Face forward with eyes closed.[4]

into the Realm of the Dead. What of Sarah that died will become clear in a sequence of ecstatic experiences that began about five months later and will be told in chapter 11.

10-8-07: My ribs started cracking and melting away, and then all my bones followed suit, leaving me feeling like a puddle on the ground. I was an amoeba pulsating to the rhythm of the drum—then dancing and growing very large. Suddenly two huge, muscular men came into the picture with something like huge wheelbarrows of clay and started throwing it onto me, handful by handful until there was a big pile of the clay. I then became aware of my backbone and was drawn, like through a drinking straw, up and into the clay, where I felt treelike. A white bird (dove?) landed on my right shoulder and a mourning dove landed on my left shoulder, and they spoke to each other by whispering into my ears.

Anyone who values their dreams enough to record them and work with their imagery and metaphors can likely attain what is intended from a ecstatic trance posture upon their very first experience with it. This is supported by the experiences of those who have attended the annual conference of the International Association for the Study of Dreams. In 2009 we tried using the Hallstatt Warrior but I did not reveal its intent beforehand. One person saw a closed casket deep down in the underbelly of a castle, and then went back upstairs to find youths running and playing, again a death-rebirth experience—motifs typical of this posture. Another person at the dream conference immediately recognized that the energy of the posture was of desolation and resurrection from the dead.

6-30-09: I had a sense of resurrecting ancient dead energies—coming out of the tomb. Clay/earth was crumbling. A left-handed warrior was put into position as we were put into the pose. His position is death. I felt a need to clear this energy about halfway through. I wondered about the safety of raising energies from the grave and began to release the pose and connect with my heart.

This journey clearly reveals an experience within the Realm of the Dead, even though the person went into the trance not knowing its intent. I have learned to expect from those who journal their dreams and appreciate such altered states of consciousness that they will in most cases accurately experience the intent of the posture.

METAMORPHOSIS POSTURES TO GAIN PERSPECTIVE

Shape-shifting is a common theme in the mythology, folklore, literature, and spiritual practices of virtually all the world's traditional cultures. In more recent times, shamanic shape-shifting stirred the imagination of a broader public beginning in the late 1960s with the publication of Carlos Castaneda's books, which focused on the culturally oriented practices of the Toltec shamans of ancient Mexico, as evinced by the seer Don Juan Matus, Carlos's teacher, who can shapeshift into a crow. In general, there are two types of shamanic shapeshifting. In one you meet your power animal and become one with it on the astral level. The other is more closely aligned with the Native American belief that you can change your physical form on the earth plane. In our posture work, changing form, as in the stages of becoming a butterfly or shape-shifting into an animal or another nonanimal living entity, are examples of what we call metamorphosis. By becoming an animal or a living or nonliving entity, we can see or experience the world from the Other's perspective, experience their reality, and learn of the world beyond ourselves, thus seeing our concerns from a new perspective.

MESOAMERICAN POWER
SHIFTING INTO DEEPER WISDOM

The Olmec are considered one of the first major civilizations of Mesoamerica, dating roughly from as early as 1500 BCE to about 400 BCE, preceding the ancient Mayan and later Aztec civilizations. The Olmec civilization is often remembered because of the gigantic stone heads that have been found at Tenochtitlán, the site of their largest city, which is on the site of present-day Mexico City.

The Olmec Prince statue was found in the area of Tabasco, Mexico, and is dated somewhere between 1100 and 600 BCE. The Olmecs were a horticultural society that sought greater control over their environment as compared to the earlier hunter-gatherer societies, thus the people of this society would likely have valued shape-shifting or transforming into animals of power. This posture typically leads a person to change into some animal or plant in order to reveal to him or her some deeper wisdom.

From my experience I have consistently found that anyone using this posture, even a novice, will experience becoming some kind of animal. My first experience with this posture and becoming a bear, related in chapter 1, was most vivid. I knew I was a bear, no question about it. The experience was one of the most powerful in my life, and from it I learned what it truly means to be "in the moment."

In November 2007, I had the opportunity to demonstrate the power of ecstatic posture work in New Paltz, New York, to the Joseph Campbell Roundtable, a group that was quite in tune with the unconscious mind through their interest in and study of ancient mythology. These novices to posture work, having gone into the Olmec Prince blind as to its shape-shifting intent, offered some amazing and reliable accounts of their experiences. One person vividly saw herself as a large cat stretching in the darkness; another person was first a cat but then became a snake, feeling its sensuous slithering as she curved herself around rocks, feeling the vibrations of the earth. A third member of

Olmec Prince Posture

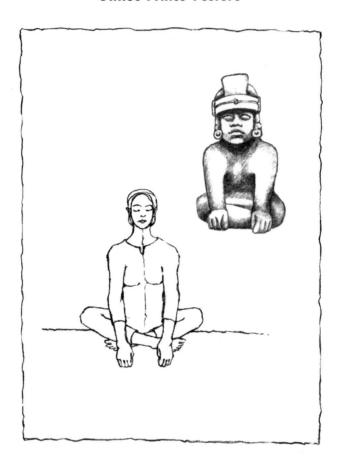

Sit on the floor with your right leg crossed in front of your left leg. Stretch your arms, with elbows locked, straight in front of you, with your fingers curled inward, toward your body, such that only the middle segment of each finger rests on the floor. Your shoulders, elbows, wrists, and knuckles are held rigid. To maintain this position you will need to lean slightly forward with your back straight, hinging from the hips. Lift your head with your closed eyes looking forward. Let your tongue protrude slightly from between your lips.

the group was again a large, panther-like cat, springing in slow motion across the ground on a gray and purple African plain. Though we did not discuss what these experiences meant to each person, the large cats represent strength and the snake wisdom, and thus it was likely that each person found new strength and for one also wisdom in these experiences.

Not all shape-shifting experiences are of animals. One person in my weekly group at home became a beanstalk, rising snakelike to infinity. The leaves were light green and perfect, with no dead or dried leaves. Susanne, who expressed a desire to pursue her spirituality, became a gargoyle on a Mayan temple. She reported in our weekly group session, "I seemed to have two consciousnesses. I had the intelligence of a rock that has lived through and experienced geological time with its recent human beings, and I had the intelligence of a watchful protector or guard animal of the pyramid," likely showing her that she has the ability to access and be the guardian of such knowledge in her pursuit of spirituality. Each of these experiences had important wisdom to reveal to each person about their own strengths and abilities, generally through some experienced characteristic of an animal, plant, or animal-like stone.

OBSERVING THE ANIMAL TEACHER

The Jama-Coaque Metamorphosis figurine (not to be confused with the Jama-Coaque Diviner, discussed in the last chapter) was found on the northern coast of Ecuador, at Jama, a market center of the ancient Jama-Coaque people. Gore reports that "our experiences with [this posture] have not been the clear transformations into animals that we associate with other metamorphosis postures. . . . It is possible that this pose mediates visceral experiences that are transformative but may be less related to animal forms."[5] This is confirmed by my own experience and my observation of others: animals are present in the trance but in close relationship to the journeyer and, as with metamorphosis postures in general, of central teaching importance. Again the person's shape may be shifted to some animal, but also to other life such as a tree or even something as inanimate as a rock. Or, a shift may not occur but the animal may be simply experienced in close proximity. I find the Olmec Prince a more comfortable posture to hold for 15 minutes so will frequently use it for the same purpose as the Jama-Coaque Metamorphosis posture. I have faith that whether I become something living or inanimate or whether I am just visited by something living or inanimate, I have something important to learn from each situation though I may not understand what I learned until some time later.

In my first two experiences with this posture, I found that with the tension in my body and arms, I was pulling on something while rocking on my buttocks, as in pulling on a rope or on the oars of a boat. This energy brought me into contact, on two different occasions, with two of my power animals. In the first experience, as I pulled on the rope, I moved into darkness; following the rope, I found at the other end one of my favorite power animals—the bear.

8-25-08: It stood up and roared. I reacted as if scared but did not feel especially scared. Then the bear started to laugh at me. I was still leery and confused. I knew I was supposed to identify with the bear. There was a fire burning in the cave but no one around it. I wondered if the bear ate them or scared them away. Part of me wanted to go sit in the bear's lap, but I was still leery. We sat side-by-side by the fire. Then I started wondering about the rope; it was tied around the bear's waist, and I realized that he knew he would get me to follow the rope to him, knowing that I am the curious type and would follow the rope. I then punched him in the shoulder, like guys do for bonding, and I laughed, too.

A little over a month later, I tried this posture again. In this experience I was paddling a canoe down Bald Eagle Creek, when three eagles

Jama-Coaque Metamorphosis Posture

Sit on the floor with your legs extended out in front of you, with feet about a foot apart, with your heels resting on the floor and your feet flexed at a right angle to your lower legs. Your bent knees are drawn up closer to your body such that you can place your right hand palm down over your right knee and your cupped left hand with fingertips bunched together resting on your left knee. Keep your spine straight, with your arms close to your body. Let your tongue protrude slightly from between your lips.

started flying along with me. One dove to catch a fish and returned to a tree along the creek, while another with a spotted head flew ahead, leading me. Then the third, also spotted, leapfrogged ahead to lead me and then landed in a tree, while the bald one took the lead. This leapfrogging continued to lead me down the creek until we came to a high stand of rocks. Each eagle had a fish and flew to its nest in a tall tree not far from the others to feed its baby eaglettes. I sat back against a rock and watched them, feeling very content and in harmony with them, knowing this is where I needed to be.

In these two stories I revisit two of my more important spirit guides. The female bear has been with me to hold me and nurture me, but this time it is a male bear showing me his strength. The eagle so far has taught me to rise above those issues that eat at me, this time she is showing me her nurturing nature. Many spirit guides I have experienced have shown me at least two sides, a side of strength that may challenge me and a side that nurtures and is gentle. Any of the postures might offer you the teaching you need at that moment though possibly each will present it in a different manner, whether through a spirit guide, a journey into some other world, through divination, or through a death-rebirth experience. In considering what the Jama Coaque Metamorphosis posture is trying to express, I consider the physicality of the posture. While sitting in that posture I feel myself pulling against my knees, rocking back on my butt as if pulling on a rope or pulling on the oars of a boat, and off balance. If my hands should slip I would likely fall backwards, a tension that could show me something unexpected.

Sarah's first experience with this posture brought her in contact with a giant clam, which she curled up inside of, transforming into a pearl.

11-10-08: I curled up into a tight ball, the shell of the giant clam closed, and it was dark. I felt hard and concentrated, like rock. Then I saw daylight again, and a woman picked me out of her mouth and plunked me down on a table. It was a restaurant, and she was yelling for the waiter. The man she was dining with looked at me and said he thought I was a pearl. When the waiter came, the woman said, horrified, "Look what was in my food!" The waiter said, "It looks like an exquisite pearl!" The woman said, "I could have broken a tooth, I want a free dinner!"

What could Sarah have learned from this experience? My first thought is that a situation may have different and even opposite meanings to different people. Opening ourselves to such different opinions can open our minds to new unexpected possibilities.

9

Attaining Self-Actualization

Using Posture Sequences to Heal Dis-ease

In attaining self-actualization we go beyond merely healing. Healing is necessary when we have a problem, be it physical or emotional, that interferes with functioning in our daily lives. Self-actualization takes us beyond the self-imposed barriers and limiting (usually unconscious) beliefs that prevent us from attaining our ultimate potential of living life authentically, creatively, and joyfully. Self-actualized people see life clearly; they are less likely to allow hopes, fears, or ego defenses to distort their observations. Self-imposed barriers and limiting beliefs may be considered emotional problems, so in this sense they are on a continuum with the dis-ease that needs to be healed. The distinction between healing and gaining self-actualization may not always be clear. Some people may claim to have no problems, but they may not be living to their full potential, thus setting a goal of attaining self-actualization may seem more acceptable to them then seeking healing.

THE IMPORTANCE OF SEQUENCING

Gaining self-actualization as well as healing is achieved in ecstatic posture work usually as a result of experiencing a sequence of postures over a period of time. The choice and order of the postures may vary, but typically we begin with a divination posture. Though we may know or think we know what is limiting us, I suggest that we leave the question open, because as we have seen in our discussion of the divination postures in chapter 6, the diviner likely knows better than our conscious mind what we need to do, what we need to work on, or the direction that we need to take. The oracle has access to and understands the metaphoric language of our unconscious mind and/or the universal mind and can tap into that to reveal to us in a very personal way what might not have occurred to us in normal consciousness; it can, in effect, mirror back to us our own truth.

The second step in facilitating self-actualization and healing is to use a spirit journeying posture into the underworld, the portal to the unconscious mind and the universal mind, to find the answer, the solution, or what we need to do to attain a goal or resolve an issue. The answers we receive from the diviner and from spirit journeying are most likely in the language of metaphor and may not be immediately understood, nor need they be, because the unconscious mind knows this language and understands it perfectly.

The third step is to allow what is learned to become integrated within ourselves, using a death-rebirth posture. Again, the experience that occurs when one takes this kind of journey is metaphoric, like much of the communication from the shamanic realm, and may not be understood by the rational mind. But with time—weeks or months, perhaps even years—the healing of problems and the growth of the self that allow one to move toward one's ultimate potential will be much in evidence, and the door to conscious understanding will have opened because of our clear intent.

These three steps may need to be repeated or rearranged in the course of pursuing a goal of greater self-actualization, because we need to allow time to integrate the messages that are coming from the personal unconscious and/or the universal mind. As well, incorporating the knowledge that is revealed through a sequence of postures is a gradual process of unfolding and may involve passing through many different layers of problems or limiting beliefs.

My first experience with working this way to intentionally achieve greater self-actualization occurred at a 2010 Cuyamungue Institute workshop on soul retrieval led by Ki Salmen. Upon returning home I found greater appreciation for this process with my own repeated use of these three steps, which led me to better understand my coyote spirit guide. My appreciation for this process grew exponentially when I extracted from my collection of more than 1,000 recorded ecstatic experiences people who had worked through a similar, basic three-stage sequence, only in these cases the journeyers did not know that these three steps comprised the basic process for attaining self-actualization. In looking back over these experiences and sharing them with the persons involved, their self-actualization has become quite evident to them.

MARIA: FINDING STRENGTH IN INDEPENDENCE

Maria's initial use of the the Nupe Mallam Diviner, a contemporary divination posture named for the Nupe Mallam tribe of sub-Saharan Africa, was reported in chapter 4. Traditionally, the Nupe Mallam shaman is consulted for help in answering questions regarding personal predicaments. Maria had been struggling to quit smoking. Though she approached her first experience with the Nupe Mallam posture blind to its intent and likely did not voice her wish to quit smoking, wanting to quit was likely on her mind. Little did she know that this experience would launch her on a journey of self-discovery that would lead to a whole new level of self-realization.

Maria's first use of this posture:

10-1-07: I began in a womb shaped, denlike cave of branches. I was trying to figure out what animal I was, then realized I was a very happy little girl, about eight years old. I was alone, but happy and free. I was in a city on a sidewalk. The city was gray and ugly, but I felt so alive and happy. I walked up a road that turned into a wide bridge in a very industrial city setting. I stayed on the bridge a while feeling happy, young, and free. Then I began

Nupe Mallam Diviner Posture

Sit with both knees bent and folded off to the right, with the knees resting on the floor. The feet point to the right, the left foot resting just to the left of the right knee. The right hand rests on the lower left leg about halfway down the calf. The left hand rests on the floor at a right angle to the body just behind the left knee, about three to five inches from the left side of the body and in line with the back of the buttocks. The left arm is rigid, supporting the weight of the upper body.

to cross the bridge and realized it led into an enormous warehouse. I did not want to go in. I turned around. Behind me was city, ugly and gray, but home. Then I got very, very sad. Then I became annoyed because I could not get off the bridge. I wanted to change visions, but that did not work. I wanted to end the meditation, but I was still on the bridge. So I let all emotion escape me and entered the warehouse. It was hell, hellish landscape. I marched through and exited the other side. I was surprised to see the road continue on a beautiful and colorful landscape. I laid down in the grass. I knew it was beautiful but I could not feel the same excitement. I was older now.

Maria returned to the next meeting of our weekly group to announce that she had not had a cigarette all week. She believed that she would have to go through hell to really quit smoking, and her brief journey through the hell of the enormous warehouse was sufficient.

Following her success in quitting smoking, Maria was encouraged to continue her work with the postures. She had just broken up with her man, Louis, a Native American who had returned to his reservation, and she was struggling to find herself. This emotional pain led her to begin a series of self-explorations using ecstatic trance work. A week after she quit smoking, we chose to use the Hallstatt Warrior, a spirit journeying posture, at our group meeting. The meaning of this experience and the one after only became clear later, in the context of her third and fourth experiences.

10-8-07: Immediately upon the start of the drumming, I knew I was standing very solidly on the edge of a high cliff. It looked like a canyon. I was not afraid. I wore a long robe and was dressed in an indigenous-looking cloth (Southwest?). As I stood there, I realized that along the canyon's circular edge we all stood (Sue, Julianne, Nick, Ron, myself, Judy, Susanne, and Sarah). We were all dressed in robes, standing apart from one another, stoically looking over the edge. Then I came back into my immediate space. I envisioned a turtle and thought, Creator, and a

voice said, "You will need this." A nondescript figure then came and put a
turtle on the ground to my left. That was the first gift. All of us raised our
palms to the sky, and when I looked out I realized everyone was receiving
gifts, though I could not see what because I was so far away from everyone
else. The second gift I received was an eagle feather fan (Sioux?). My first
thought was concern: This does not belong to me! But it was like the air
itself told me it was okay. Then Louis showed up. He walked up to my right
side and said he couldn't stay, but he would be back when my self-work
was done and his was, too. I asked him how I could believe that, and he set
a large rock down at my right and walked away. Then we all turned from
the cliff and walked away in separate directions.

The theme of Maria's independence clearly begins to emerge in this experience. A little over a month later, she journeyed with the Olmec Prince, a shape-shifting posture, which defined something needed in her personal growth. As she entered her trance, she found she was a horse standing in a field, cooling off from a run, with the rest of her herd standing around her. When a black mustang who had been leading the herd resumed running, all the horses, herself included, followed. Maria recorded, "I felt power. I thought, We are/I am only as strong as he (the leader) is." Maria found this strength through identifying with a powerful mustang. She kept up with the mustang and felt the freedom of running. The mustang provided Maria with validation. Meeting the mustang led her to find her capacity, her talents, and her creativity encouraging her in living independently, without a male figure to depend upon. But that was not all; Maria's journey had only just begun. The Tlazolteotl healing posture she tried next helped bring her experiences together and gave her something to be treasured.

12-10-07: Immediately I became a cat, like in the Broadway musical
Cats. *I had pointed ears and an exaggeratedly long and bushy tail. I felt*
playful and sassy. Then it was just me on a small pier. I was pulling a thick

rope out of the ocean. It was very hard work, and I pulled and pulled for a long time. Finally, I pulled up a brown chest. I dragged it onto the pier and cut the rope. Inside was lots of treasure! On the lid was a picture of a pirate, and I reached up and pulled out a gold statue of a seated cat. Then I was the upright, tall, sassy golden cat. After looking at my treasure awhile, I stood at the edge of the pier and stared stoically out to sea. Then I saw the woman I was in an earlier meditation, standing on the edge of a canyon. Same pose, same feeling. Then I saw the horse in a field that I was in another meditation. Same pose, same feeling. The three of us stood solidly for a long time, with energy moving in a triangle/circle. Suddenly, the cat reached for the treasure chest and left. The canyon woman picked up her gifts and walked away. The horse threw back her head and began to trot. All of these are me. I think of culmination and completion!

The culmination of a process and the attainment of a new level of self-actualization is often reflected in experiencing feelings of bliss. Maria felt a new strength, even though she had separated from her man and knew she desired a long-term relationship. She wanted to consolidate and internalize her changes with a rebirth, and so a few months later she used the Feathered Serpent.

3-31-08: First, I was aware of a very tall man standing behind me. He placed his hands on my shoulders, and the feeling was secure, reassuring, not oppressive. He told me (without words) that I was safe. Then I noticed how solid and secure I felt on my own. It felt good to have his reassurance. I stood there a long time. Then my belly began to grow. I literally felt my stomach grow until I was the size of a nine-month pregnant woman. I even opened my eyes during the session once because it felt so real. Then a strong, brilliant sun shone down on us. Light and sparkles covered us like a spotlight. It all felt so easy, happy, content, warm, and eventually blissful. I was so happy I wanted to invite my friends and family into the light. Slowly, they gathered around. I, very pregnant, and with this man still behind me, took a bouquet of bright flowers and started handing them out to family

and friends. Each time I gave someone a flower, the color of their clothes,
skin, hair—everything—became enhanced and very bright.

The tall man saying she was safe, the feeling of bliss, and the celebration with bright colors show that Maria has incorporated her sense
of strength in her independence. The pregnancy though, seems to have
a mixed meaning—it seems that her bliss is because she is pregnant.
However, although she does want to have a child, that does not seem
to be in her immediate future. In this experience her pregnancy seems
likely to be metaphoric for feeling fulfilled in her life as it is, representing her feminine strength of independence. Maria's stories go beyond
the healing of her limitations; they illustrate the power of using the postures sequentially, over a period of time, to effect a whole new level of
self-actualization.

One may note that the postures used in this sequence do not specifically follow the order of divination, underworld, death-rebirth.
These experiences occurred over two years before I even considered
the importance of a sequence, and they were not examined as a possible sequence leading to change at the time. A divination posture (the
Nupe Mallam Diviner) led Maria to quit smoking. Then, in working
toward feeling strength in her independence, the sequence began with
a Realm of the Dead posture (the Hallstatt Warrior), followed by a
shape-shifting posture (the Olmec Prince), then the cleansing posture
of Tlazolteotl, ending with the death-rebirth posture of the Feathered
Serpent. I frequently use the analogy of peeling the layers of an onion.
There may be many different layers in overcoming a problem,such as
Maria's case of feeling abandoned by Louis. Growing past each layer
involves understanding the issue of the layer (through divination), of
uncovering the solution (through journeying to the underworld), and
then incorporating the solution (by experiencing death-rebirth or shape
shifting). I expect that at the intermediate stages of the process of
change, the person goes through some of these steps without the need
of a specific ecstatic trance experience—a nighttime dream, or some

other experience, such as seeing something in a movie, hearing it in a song, or talking to a friend, may provided what is needed to facilitate this change. It is also sometimes possible that a posture may address one of these stages even if it does not specifically match the intent, as there is much fluidity in the purposes of the postures.

Maria had been dependent upon cigarettes as well as upon Louis. Her warehouse experience may have opened both doors, but it took her a while longer to deal with the hell of losing Louis. The Hallstatt Warrior followed by the Olmec Prince experience of becoming a powerful horse was the first layer of transformation, but to complete the process she needed something more, cleansing and then another death-rebirth transformation that went beyond simply feeling strong like the mustang to a celebration of the feeling of being fulfilled. I am offering this explanation as a possibility with the understanding that much of the process is unconscious and we will likely not know the steps. I do have faith that these postures are very powerful in accessing the unconscious mind and the universal mind and can produce such change without the need of such conscious explanation.

JEN: OVERCOMING
FEELINGS OF INADEQUACY

Jen hosted a new ecstatic posture group in Huntingdon, a town about 50 miles from where I live, as a result of the one hour workshop I offered at the college in that town. I traveled to this town once a week over the next several months until the end of the school year when many in the group left for the summer. Following are six of Jen's ecstatic experiences. The postures were selected not specifically as a healing sequence, but to teach the power of the individual posture to this new group. We began with the Olmec Prince posture, a relatively simple and comfortable metamorphosis posture that generally offers a fairly vivid but nonthreatening experience. Jen did not understand the significance of this her first experience with ecstatic posture journeying until a few weeks later when we returned to her initial experience and examined it in relationship to her next several ecstatic experiences. When she realized that her snarling and growing teeth, as described in her experience with the Olmec Prince that follows, represented her strength and determination to overcome limiting feelings about herself, she recognized it as an experience that gave her the strength to face the experiences that followed.

12-2-09: I had a sense of groundedness and eventually a physical twitching in my cheeks that invited my lips to lift. Then I began to feel like my teeth were growing and my cheeks wanted to smile or snarl. Then I had a strong awareness, and the twitching turned to tingling at my navel center, which became a vision of my umbilical cord. After the rattling ended the session, I felt I could not move from the posture, perhaps because my energy and attention were so grounded. I did not want to be removed from the experience. Now I feel kind of shaky from the inside out.

A week later, Jen took a question about the nature of what was limiting or inhibiting her life to the Mayan Oracle, a divination posture we introduce here. A small pottery figure of the Mayan Oracle can be found in the Princeton University Art Museum. This figurine originates from the classical Mayan civilization that flourished in Mexico during the sixth and eighth centuries CE. When questions and concerns are taken to this diviner, her answers are simple and practical—like "Let go and stop trying so hard"—yet given in a supportive way.

In her experience with the Mayan Oracle, Jen said that the drumming during the session surrounded her and tunneled through her. She asked the oracle the question "How can I help my yoga business grow to pay my rent?" She recorded, "I had no visuals or physical experiences other than the vibrations in and around me." Several days later, I e-mailed Jen, suggesting that she explore the feelings of tunneling vibrations more: "If this were my experience, I would examine how the surrounding and tunneling vibrations around me felt. For example it could have been a comforting blanket that provides me with a sense

Mayan Oracle Posture

Sit on the floor cross-legged, with your right leg crossed in front of the left. Your left foot is tucked under your right thigh so that it extends beyond the right side of your body. Your right hand rests on the outside of your left knee, with the fingers together and thumb held away from the fingers. Your left arm is bent at the elbow and held away from the body, with the left hand raised, wrist slightly tilted toward your face, and hand, thumb, and fingers cupped into a C with the palm turned toward your face. You face forward, with your eyes closed and lips slightly parted.

of security, suggesting that I can trust the future, or maybe something I could provide my clients for them to feel warm and secure. On the other hand, the vibrations could possibly be bad vibrations that have been limiting me."

Two weeks after that experience, Jen used the Feathered Serpent death-rebirth posture and experienced herself as the Tree of Life.

12-30-10: The first part of the journey invited me into a body of water. It had a tunnel-like pull, bringing my body deeper into the water. I then began to sway, a circular sway. I was able to see a sandy, mucky, quicksand floor in the body of water. I then realized I was a tree rooted in a swamp. My roots (feet) remained grounded, and my body swayed more. This time the tunnel spiraled, lifting my trunk upward. I felt stable and flowing. Then a bright full moon shone on me, and I saw the tunnel, more like a V-shaped energy field coming down through the crown of my head and filling my limbs. A feeling of being stuck, with an openness that more is possible, came to me. If I could uplift my roots I could remove myself from the mucky swamp and spiral into a higher consciousness without losing the groundedness of my roots. Maybe I need to uproot?

Several days later I offered Jen the following thoughts. "The Feathered Serpent takes us through the cycle of death and rebirth. Its intent is to first enter a womblike place, perhaps a cave, a warm, dark environment—the swamp in which you found yourself. After resting there awhile, you then rose to a new life. Your experience matches well the intent of the posture, with the body of water and tunnel-womb. You are somewhat stuck there, but the energy is pulling up on you for rebirth or new life. It does seem to describe your struggle well."

A week later Jen used the Priestess of Malta, a spirit journeying posture to the Middle World. She reported: "Again, circular swaying, grounded, all feelings were in the navel center and the heart center. The number 6, hearts, and leaves were flowing from my heart center." During that session, Jen mentioned that she had gained several new students during the past week and consequently felt more confident about the sustainability of her yoga business. She suggested that this experience seemed right—that this flow of hearts and leaves from her heart represented some resolution of the issue that she had been struggling with. In my e-mail I expressed curiosity, asking if she had done something different. "Last week you were stuck in the swamp and wanted to lift your roots to free yourself. Did you do something different to free yourself?" Jen responded that she had "let go of numbers," of worrying about the number of people attending her classes and the money coming in. That had freed her to focus more supportively on her students. She felt that this change in attitude had made a difference.

In considering the sequence of postures that led to this change, we see that Jen began with a metamorphosis posture that gave her teeth with which to fight. The divination posture then suggested that her vibrations needed to be considered. This consideration led her to a death-rebirth experience of struggling to break free of mud, a change that was validated in the Middle World journey of hearts and leaves flowing from her heart. These experiences point to a resolution of Jen's fear concerning the sustainability of her yoga business, but they also gave her new strength to face a deeper problem, which was the source of her fear. In the following experience, the Jama-Coaque Diviner showed Jen the source of her deep-seated feelings of inadequacy.

1-27-11: Visions/memories surfaced. In second grade my barrette fell from my hair and I lost it. I cried in the bathroom until my teacher comforted me. In the seventh grade, my art teacher saw paint spilled on the floor. She let everyone continue painting and creating but made me clean up the paint even though I had not spilled it. I felt she asked me to clean it up because my stick figure art was inadequate compared to the others. In the fifth grade, I was often made fun of because I sat up straight. In the twelfth grade my boyfriend physically and mentally abused me. I asked the diviner to unleash me to witness why I have low self-esteem, why I do not

appreciate my little bit of creativity, and why I always feel inadequate. My
left eye swelled up and itched as though I was going to cry.

With the understanding that these incidents in Jen's early years had instilled her feelings of inadequacy, she used the Jivaro South American Lower World posture on her next journey the following week. Before we continue with Jen's experience, I will introduce this spirit journeying posture.

The Jivaro South American Lower World posture was found in Ecuador by Michael Harner and presented in his book *The Way of the Shaman*. The Jivaro were famous because of their skill of shrinking heads. In the case of this particular posture, the Lower World is entered easily by many different ways, such as through a cave, tunnel, flower, vulva, stairs, hollow tree, slide, chute, or water; often there is a flow of turbulence, whether of swirling energy or of water.

At the next meeting of our new weekly ecstatic trance group, Jen bravely journeyed to the underworld to find answers to her questions.

2-3-11: I immediately revisited the physical location of my "close call" today while driving. While there, I felt an openness and a closing above me. I felt a soft hovering and wings closing in around me, protecting me. As I began to let go of this vision, my body softened, and I began to move deep through the earth to the sea. I felt and saw myself swirling as a sea turtle, swimming happily in a protective shell and lots of room for movement in my body. I gazed left at the cavern and it glistened with many colors.

There are two levels to this experience: first, feeling protected from the near-accident Jen had experienced earlier that day; and second, protection for the much younger school-age Jen from those incidents that she had experienced on her previous trance journey and had interpreted as being the root of her feelings of inadequacy. Her adult self now has the strength to be able to go back and offer her younger self the protection she needs. At either level she found protective wings and then a

Jivaro South American Lower World Posture

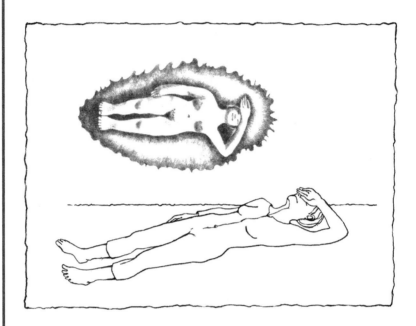

Lie on the floor with the back of your head resting comfortably against the floor. Your right arm is beside your body in a natural, relaxed position. Your left arm is raised, with the back of your left hand resting on the middle of your forehead without pressure on the eyes.

protective shell, yet at the same time she had the freedom of movement that is so important to her.

Three months after the beginning of her journey of self-exploration, Jen used the transformative Jama-Coaque Metamorphosis posture with stellar results, as she achieved her goal of rising above her feelings of inadequacy in the flowing movement of an American Indian eagle dance.

2-17-11: I arrived at a desert-like clearing. I felt my right hand and arm tingling, then vibrating, as though the beads inside the rattle were in my forearm. I glanced down to see it shaking. It felt as though all of us in the circle were each shaking rattles in our right hand. My image then became a winged person dancing to the left halfway, and to the right halfway, like a Native American dancer wearing large wings. This dancer continued to move, kicking up dust and sand and then lowering to the Earth and spiraling as it rose skyward.

Thus the sequence began with divination to uncover the source of Jen's feeling of inadequacy, which led to her journey into the Lower World, where she found protection from that which made her feel inadequate. This experience gave Jen the strength for a transformative rebirth, allowing her to rise skyward with a sense of freedom, moving beyond her feelings of inadequacy. With this final experience, Jen felt a new level of self-confidence, both in herself and in what she is doing in life.

JUDITH: LETTING GO OF GUILT AND GRIEF

Judith had been struggling to deal with trying to detach from the problems of her adult daughter, who lived at a distance from her. She was experiencing considerable chest pain and insomnia as a result. Through a healing circle, she had found clarity about the need to let go of her feelings of grief and guilt about letting her daughter work out her problems on her own, without Mom's interference. But letting go does not happen overnight and can take months, if not years. Knowing that one has the right to let go or that it is healthy to let go is one thing; allowing that concept to become integrated on a feeling level is another matter. The following ecstatic trance experiences helped Judith in her process of detaching from her daughter with grace. She started out with a journey to the underworld, using the Jivaro South American posture.

9-10-07: At first I was very aware of the weight of my arm on my head in the posture. I felt my face as though it were a mask with huge teeth and a stretched-out mouth. Slowly, my arm seemed to go into my head, and as that happened I began to be aware of a round, live, moving life growing under my left hand, moving my fingers into a cuplike roundness, pulsing life, growing bigger. I was suddenly aware that my whole body cavity from the chest down was empty. It felt like a big serving dish. The life in the left hand grew and moved. I wondered what it was. I tried not to think, but just kept on relaxing and felt the experience. I could not discern what the life in the left hand was, only that it was alive, powerful, and big.

In this journey into the underworld, Judith found the heaviness of dealing with her daughter's problems in the weight of her arm; she felt like an empty serving dish, emptied by giving and giving. At the same time she experienced the strength to let go of her guilt and grief as an unknown growing form that she held in the palm of her hand, as if it was well within reach.

In her next trance experience, Judith went to the Realm of the Dead using the Hallstatt Warrior. She recorded: "I had feelings of abundance and great heat. . . . I decided to use some of that energy to send to my daughter, who is very sick." This abundance of heat, a sign of the presence of healing energy, gave Judith the strength to withstand the heaviness of her situation as well as a quantity of energy that she could share with her daughter. In letting go of her grief and guilt by not feeling responsible for her daughter's well-being, she found greater energy for herself, and could extend that newfound energy to her daughter without engaging in old, dysfunctional patterns.

Finally, with the Feathered Serpent, she was able to affirm her changes and experience a rebirth.

11-5-07: I had a light show—it was as if there were these awesome colors drawing me out into the cosmos. At first there was a beautiful blue, a rather dark blue, but lit up inside; then it was surrounded by aquamarine, and it slowly changed into magentas and purples. I thought I was being drawn into the cosmos—as I thought about it, I could say like the Aurora Borealis, but when I thought that, the colors became all murky and un-bright. I consciously tried not to think, just let go, and once more the color show came over me, only this time it was light yellows, turquoises, and pinks.

The process of letting go of grief and guilt takes time. Giving and giving endlessly to a loved one, and the feelings of guilt and grief that come when one tries to detach, can drain one's strength and energy, leaving one feeling heavy and as empty as an empty serving dish. It takes time to replace these ingrained patterns with the more spontaneous feeling of giving freely, which makes one feel strong and more energized. With these new feelings to support a new life direction, the colors of Judith's life brighten and become vibrant.

In considering the sequence of postures from divination, through journeying into the underworld, and to a death-rebirth experience, I at times have ended this sequence with an additional experience of journeying into the upper world, to celebrate the rebirth. Judith's upper world experience might have been even more vivid if an upper world posture had been used, rather than the death-rebirth Feathered Serpent posture.

10

A Cycle of Physical and Emotional Healing

A New Perspective on Cancer and Life

A NEW PERSPECTIVE ON CANCER

While a number of postures have been determined to be specifically healing postures including the Bear Spirit, Tlazolteotl, The Couple of Cernavoda and the Chiltan Spirits postures, most any, if not all, the postures can promote healing as is evident in this next sequence of eight ecstatic experiences, beginning and ending with Hallstatt Warrior experiences. However, even though all of these experiences promoted healing, each had elements that matched the intent of the posture. At this point in our exploration of these postures we as a group were not selecting them for specific purposes and intent, and I was not selecting them specifically to help me in the healing of my cancer. Yet, since the cancer was foremost in my mind, each posture and each experience that follows finds its own way to help in healing. The Hallstatt posture used in the next weekly group session was likely selected the week before because of our curiosity about how the posture would be experienced.

In one of my earliest experiences in dealing with my prostate cancer, I found the Hallstatt Warrior of great comfort. I had just learned that my PSA score was elevated and my doctor had ordered a biopsy of my prostate. Naturally, I was worried.

3-11-08: I was cold, hugging myself for warmth. Walking through a dark, damp forest with tall trees above me, I come to a shallow, moss-covered cave. I sit down with my back against the rock wall hugging myself. The wall opens, and I am pulled down backward into a deep cave. I see a big fire in the middle with a ring of shadowy natives dancing around it. The natives put me on a stone block in the middle of and above the fire and they continue to dance. The block slowly rises up, lifting me higher and higher through the top of the cave, to where I am again outside above the trees and the cave—standing, looking out across the world in the warm sunlight.

This was a journey from the desolation of worry, to visiting the "natives" deep in a cave, and to a hopeful return to a new world of warm sunlight—a journey that gave me great hope and comfort at the time. It matches well the intent of the Hallstatt Warrior, beginning in a place of desolation and going into the spirit world (though I called them natives at this time) before being reborn into the warm sunlight. This was the first of eight ecstatic experiences using five different postures that led me through the first sequence of several in dealing my cancer. Another sequence to overcome what was eating at me will follow in the next section of this chapter. As this first sequence evolves, I discover or realize that these "natives" are really healing spirits, and they will be joined by a bear, the Bear Spirit with all of its healing powers of both nurturance and strength. The next experience, using the Feathered Serpent death-rebirth posture, occurred two days before I received the diagnosis of fairly advanced cancer.

3-24-08: I'm standing on the mountaintop where the last experience ended when a section of the earth under me starts going down like an elevator, lowering me into the cave. I am again within the circle of fire with shadowy spirits dancing around outside the fire. In their dance they start throwing something at me that feels sort of like sand. I am naked and it feels cleansing.
Then they stop throwing the sand but continue to dance. I start

dancing in place, turning in a circle—sort of the Native American dance
step of toe, heel. Then I stop. I'm sweating profusely. Sweat flows off me. I
begin to rise up again to the top of the cave and out to the mountaintop. I
stand naked in the cold air for a while and it feels good. Then someone, a
woman, a spirit maiden, comes up behind me and wraps me in a bearskin.

The experience of the spirits throwing sand at me, which I believe
was a precognition of knowing that I had cancer, well fits the intent of
death and rebirth of the Feathered Serpent—the death of going into
the lower world and then being reborn as I rise up and meet the spirit
maiden. Again as these ecstatic experiences evolve, what was then sand
soon became sparks that entered my body to destroy the cancer cells.

I was well aware of the ground breaking research of Carl Simonton
in the 1970s who demonstrated how cancer cells can be destroyed
through the use of mental imagery. He would have his cancer patients
imagine some image such as Pac Man or a white polar bear (metaphoric
for white blood cells), enter their bodies to gobble up and destroy the
cancer cells. At the time of the publication of Simonton's book, *Getting*
Well Again, I was active in the American Association for the Study of
Mental Imagery (AASMI), and a few years later would become president of the association. With this interest, I had attended a couple of
workshops led by Carl Simonton. I also participated in other workshops
led by Bernie Siegel who wrote *Love, Medicine and Miracles,* a book of
stories of cancer patients healing themselves, and president of AASMI
a couple of years before me. I have great faith in the power of the use of
mental imagery and the healing mind.

The bear spirit comes into my next ecstatic experience again led by
the Hallstatt Warrior. I likely chose to use the Hallstatt Warrior posture, because of the power I felt in using it on previous occasions. By
the time of this experience I had received verification of the diagnosis.

3-31-08: A bear appears between my legs, and I grasp onto the fur of
her back. She carries me to her cave where she sits back on her rear and

holds me—she feels very warm and comfortable in the darkness. The bear motions with her head to look down a side tunnel to her left to where I can again see the spirits dancing around a fire in a circle. I go there briefly where the spirits are dancing around me and throw sparks at me.

I am then back with the bear, cuddling into her fur, and I start nursing off her tit. Then the spirits are dancing around us and sparks are flying into the air around us. I feel very nurtured by the bear. The Hallstatt Warrior posture took me back to the same place it has taken me before because that place seems to be where my unconscious tells me I need to go for the work I am doing on my cancer.

Now that I had felt the healing of this spirit guide, the bear, I asked my wife, Toni, to hold me as I was held by the Bear Spirit as we listened to 15 minutes of drumming.

4-7-08: I feel the pings of the drumming, the energy of the Bear Spirit, attacking my cancer cells and killing them. I feel Toni low on my back as a little bear. I feel very planted and stable with her warmth and weight against my back.

Then in our next Monday evening group meeting, Sarah held me similarly, again using the Bear Spirit posture.

4-7-08: I feel her warmth. Then three different bear experiences occur:

The first bear—I feel myself in Lejra, Denmark at the remains of King Hrothgar's great hall lying naked on the grass—focusing my attention as a berserker.

The second bear—I am dancing wearing a bear skin with the bear head over my head—moving in the Native American dance type—but more frenzied.

The third bear—I feel the sinew of a bear—feel myself standing with muscles bulging—showing their sinew. I feel my knees slightly bent and planted, but standing as a bear, being held from behind by a she bear.

All three bear experiences made me feel strong—whereas before the bear holding me was soft and nurturing. The first and last images of this experience need some elaboration.

First, in my first book *Grendel and His Mother: Healing the Traumas of Childhood Through Dreams, Imagery and Hypnosis*, I recognize that each line of the Old English poem of Beowulf is meaningful in describing the process of overcoming our tormentor, Grendel. In continuing my research and fascination for this ancient story that takes place in Denmark, I had the opportunity to visit Lejra, Denmark in 2004, and find what some consider the remains of King Hrothgar's great hall. In this story of, the hero, Beowulf, lies down naked in the great hall waiting for the king's tormentor, Grendel, to enter. When Grendel enters, Beowulf jumps up and grabs Grendel's arm, tearing it off in the great struggle. Facing our tormentor requires us to let down all our defenses, thus to be naked. I returned again to this archeological site in 2006 with my wife, where I re-enacted Beowulf by lying down in the remains of the hall. It was the above ecstatic experience that led me to understand that Beowulf was a berserker, a word that comes from the old Norse word meaning bearskin. The berserkers were those special warriors who would work themselves up into a fighting frenzy to feel invulnerable and who would fight naked. A king often had twelve berserkers among his retainers.

The third experience, that of the sinew of the bear, is from the story of Loki's Children, which is also the title of my second book (unpublished). Again an ancient myth, the Prose Edda, outlines the course of therapy in facing our guilt. In this myth, one of the six magical substances used to restrain Fenrir, the ever-growing wolf, our obsessive worry, is the sinew of a bear.

Whereas in the earlier experience the bear was female and nurturing, in this experience I learned and felt the strength of the male bear. Each bear spirit, whether the bearskin berserker, the frenzied Native American bear dancer, or the muscular sinew of the bear gave me the strength to face the worry about my cancer, while the nurturance of the female bear spirit gave me emotional support and comfort.

In this next experience I called upon Tlazolteotl to aid in cleansing me of the cancer.

4-14-08: I am holding something in my hands against my chest—I think it is an offering. It is warm. I think it could be a rabbit or cat, then it starts purring—I can feel the purr against my chest—the cat was asleep, then it wakes and jumps out of my hands. As I go after it, I notice I am in a simple cool, dark room—orangish walls with several lit candles and an altar in front of me. Behind the altar a priestess with a Mayan headdress is sitting on the floor. As I go after the cat, it runs and jumps into her lap.

I then see the shadowy spirits dancing around me—they usher me around to the right of the priestess, ducking through a low door into a back room. We sit on the floor and again they start throwing sparks at me— first one spirit, then another. I can feel the sparks hit me and go inside me in sort of a fizzing way—the sparks are healing.

Tlazolteotl, the cleansing healer, brought me back to the healing spirits who continue to throw sparks to cleanse me of my cancer cells. As this journey continued, I next visited the Venus of Galgenberg, a Sky World posture, who also brought me back to the spirits, six days before my surgery.

5-6-08: I am sitting on a hilltop—the fields are open around me—it is night and I am facing the full moon. I see silhouette spirit figures passing in front of the moon and feel them circling around me. Then I feel their presences sitting in a circle around me, all facing the moon as I am. They begin to sway from side to side and Om. We are all Oming.

I then think of IxChel—the Mayan moon goddess and the goddess of illness—who, as a goddess, brings the community together around someone in need of healing.

The spirits do not throw the sparks and I do not feel a need for them to do so. I am just comforted being in their company while we appreciate the moon of the Sky World and the Mayan moon goddess who brings the community together.

Then at our next group meeting after my surgery, I returned to the Hallstatt Warrior, who seemed to bring this sequence to a close.

6-2-08: I'm standing on the hilltop, holding a bear cape around me. The spirits from my previous experiences are dancing at a distance and not throwing their sparks at me. I get down on all fours and I am the bear—or at least watching the bear—as it walks away slowly, going up the road to the ridge and along the ridge, around the rocks at the end of the ridge and into the cave in the rocks (a shallow cave on the ridge behind our house that I have known of for years). I have the feeling of completion, that the spirits initially introduced to me by the Hallstatt Warrior have done their job.

I still had ahead of me a series of radiation treatments, radiation that I visualized as sparks being shot into me to destroy any remaining cancer cells. Three years later, after this radiation, I continue to be clear of cancer.

A PERSONAL STORY OF A SELF-ACTUALIZATION AND HEALING

Finally, my personal story about using the postures for self-actualization and healing.

I recognized that one barrier to my self-actualization involved an issue that was eating away at me in my relationship with my wife, Toni; it concerned how I would react at times to what she might say or the way she might say it. I didn't like it, but I have found it difficult to overcome this pattern. As the following series of ecstatic experiences developed, it became apparent that this issue was related to our increased togetherness since my wife's retirement five years ago and my reaction to some of her behaviors, all of which amount to patterns of reactivity in our dance of life together. Moreover, this dysfunctional pattern in my own life, I came to realize, was part of a more immediate problem, which confronted me in March of 2008 when I was diagnosed with prostate cancer. Over a period of two years I used the postures to address my healing, which became a profound journey of self-actualization. This journey had two dimensions. One dimension was of the ecstatic experiences of spirits throwing sparks at me to destroy my cancer cells, but the even bigger dimension was to let go of what was eating at me, both in terms of my cancer and my life in general. It was this second dimension or journey that would change my life at a much deeper level.

This series of experiences began with the Olmec Prince, a shape-shifting posture that gave me a powerful animal spirit guide. It began with my pursuit to find my east medicine shield, the shield of our winged brethren that represents, to me, the intellectual part of myself. But it ended up also being the beginning of my journey to overcome what was eating at me. I chose to pursue my east medicine shield, because I had recently found my west shield in my relationship with the healing bear, as seen above, and the east would give me the balance I felt I needed with the west, the balance between the rational and the emotional, a balance I needed in overcoming cancer. Because east is represented by the birds, I chose to hold feathers between my fingers while in the posture as a prop to deepen my trance. In my first experience (5-23-08), I became a hummingbird perched on the Rose of Sharon outside our kitchen window, and I was looking in through the window. I saw me with my head on the table, looking depressed and alone. My wife came in and started rubbing my shoulders. She then sat in the other chair and reached out to hold my arm. Then she stood and pulled me up to hug me.

With this experience of feeling Toni's support in mind, I continued on my journey five days later to find my east medicine shield, again using the Olmec Prince, and again holding the feathers in my fingers.

5-27-08: I was both myself and an eagle soaring above Coburn [where we live]. I was watching Toni and me in the garden. She was in her vegetable garden, and I was out with the blueberries. Toni called to me to turn on the pump to fill the water barrel and I came over. I then saw the eagle and I lay down on the grass, watching it watch me. I lay still and felt very content, such that the eagle came down closer and closer. Finally it landed beside me, watching me, and I watched it. We felt secure together. I wondered what it was trying to say to me.

The eagle provided me with the representative of my east shield, but even more important was the recognition that this was a journey of letting go of what was eating at me, a journey toward feeling content. As I dwelt on this experience over the next week, the message of the eagle became clear: that it was important to me to be part of nature, to let go of control, and to be in harmony, showing patience and accepting things as they are. Again I used the Olmec Prince with feathers.

6-2-08: I was lying on the ground with the eagle sitting next to me. I could see green energy coming out of its eyes, flowing to me. The energy made me sit up. It awakened me. I then could hear a wood thrush saying something like "wake up," almost frantically, over and over. It lasted several minutes. Then I could hear the tree frogs chirping, sounds I rarely hear because of my deafness, especially with background noise such as the drumming. My calling of the eagle to sit by me required me to show patience, letting go of control, understanding and being part of nature, and accepting things as they are.

Two months later, I was able to thank the eagle for his message, again using the Olmec Prince. In the trance I see my eagle flying in circles and myself lying on the ground. I tell him how beautiful he is, and he pecks at his wing and drops a feather for me. I have a stick I have been whittling and give it to the eagle. He then flies away, and I hurry to keep him in sight. When I get to the post office, where I can clearly see the mountain ridge, I see him fly to a large tree near the end of the ridge over the creek. I start thinking about what kind of place, a platform or something, I can leave things on for him to eat, dead mice, or groundhogs, or fish, and where I should put it, near the creek, but where I can see it from my window, high, so other animals can't get at the food. I have since built two such platforms at the end of our yard beyond the garden. Twice since then I have seen eagles perched nearby. Once again, the eagle was teaching me to let go of my need to control, and to live in harmony with nature, and especially with my wife.

My experiences with the eagle continued. Several experiences later using the Olmec Prince I learned to laugh at my human foibles by trying to fly, as well as to value giving to others, important next steps in letting go of control.

> *8-22-08: I am an eagle sitting on a branch above the creek, my head darting back and forth watching for a fish. I see one and easily take off, skimming the water and catching the fish. Also at the same time I feel myself as a human, panic, throw my arms everywhere in taking off, and miss the fish. I then fly up over the garden and drop the fish in front of Toni. She looks up, smiles, and buries the fish under the seeds she was planting. She goes to find me to tell me what happened.*

The eagle has been a central figure in many of my ecstatic experiences, but the message from my spirit bird became the clearest when I used the Jama-Coaque Diviner. In this experience, he told me, through the message of the eagle, to "go with the flow" and "rise above it all," an experience I recounted earlier in chapter 2. In situations that trigger deep emotions, integrating is much is easier said than done. The most effective way is through such avenues as hypnosis and shamanic ecstatic experiences. The attitude of "go with the flow" and "rise above it" finally became integrated for me with the following experience, again using Olmec Prince.

> *1-23-11: I sat in front of the Olmec Prince in a jungle clearing in Mexico. A black panther sat next to him in same posture. It stretched with its hind*

end up and head down, and then came over to sniff around me before wandering off into the jungle. I started following him on all fours. We came to a pond, and he lapped up some water. So did I, and in looking into the pond, I saw my reflection—black face with green eyes. When I looked up, the other panther was gone. I wandered off, saw a rabbit, and batted at it with little interest. I wandered back to the Olmec Prince. I had an attitude of being above it all—the attitude the eagle was trying to show me. Thus, I finally made it.

Achieving greater emotional detachment from what was "eating at me," of letting go of my need to be in control, gave me greater freedom to be creative, thanks to the experiences I just described. But this was not the end of my transformation. In another round of ecstatic experiences, the coyote brought me to another level of self-actualization, one that allowed me to be able to laugh at what had been troubling me. My first experience occurred at the soul-retrieval workshop at the Cuyamungue Institute with Ki Salmen, where we first used the Tlazolteotl cleansing posture with no specific intention in mind.

8-26-10: Ki's rattle divided, and I heard a deeper sound from behind her at the wall of the kiva saying, "Tell me, tell me," over and over. Tlazolteotl wanted me to reveal something. I was sweating profusely the entire fifteen minutes until the end of the session. I now think what I was supposed to do was to let go of my expectations or needs of Toni in all ways.

That night at the Cuyamungue Institute, in the desert of Pojoaque Pueblo, north of Santa Fe, I heard the coyotes howling.

The next day, in our divination quest with the Olmec Diviner, I approached the oracle with the questions, "Can I do the journey for myself? How many soul parts am I to retrieve? And which power animal or guiding spirit can help?" These questions were proposed by Ki, and I continued without the thought of what I was seeking to heal, though I am sure that the issue of my need to control was still alive within me. The answers became evident in the following experience.

8-27-10: I found the diviner sitting under a tree. With a motion of his head he beckoned me to sit down beside him. This action told me that I could do the journey for myself. I looked to him with the question of how many parts I was seeking. He indicated to me to listen by putting his right hand behind his ear. As I listened, a coyote yipped and howled. Then a second coyote yipped and howled. Then a third one yipped with no howl. I looked at him perplexed, and he just shrugged his shoulders. In this journey the coyote is to be my power animal.

On the third day of the workshop, using the Jivaro South American posture to journey into the Lower World, I sought to recover the missing parts of my soul, whether two or three.

8-28-10: I slid out the top of my head and along the ground outside the kiva. As I glided along the ground on my back, a coyote was pawing at me. To get away from its paw, I floated up onto a tree branch. There I saw I was in a native village with grass huts in a circle. I floated down to lie on the ground with the native dancers dancing around me. I was not the only one. We, all nine of us [i.e., workshop attendees], were there lying in a circle with our feet toward the center, where a fire was smoking. Between us here and there were geysers of smoke rising from the ground, and several coyotes were jumping around from geyser to geyser, pawing at them as if to try to stop them, but when the coyotes left my geysers of smoke, I was able to breathe in the smoke from two or three geysers. They felt cool, like a cool breeze, but smelled of smoke. Then I found myself back in my body with the cool breeze, in the kiva.

At this point I did not know what to make of these experiences, the meaning only became clear later. That afternoon on the last day of the workshop, a transformation posture, the corn goddess, was to be used in order to let these recovered soul parts become integrated. This posture requires that I sit on my heels, which I am not able to do, so I switched to the Olmec Prince Metamorphosis posture and found myself at the two spots at Cuyamungue where I like to go to meditate. Once again, my coyote friend was there.

8-28-10: I found myself at both my power spots at Cuyamungue and at the spot beside the road. I was a mouse looking up at me. I could feel my nose twitching as I was squeaking out, "Don't ignore me, don't ignore me," over and over—"Don't ignore me as you did for so many years." Then I/ we noticed a coyote to our right. He first put his face right against mine, then turned his back to me, repeating this sequence of gestures over and over. I understood this as the coyote making fun of me and again telling me, "Don't take yourself so seriously."

These soul-retrieval experiences felt powerful and significant, yet it would take several more months for me to make some sense out of these experiences. Part of me felt the experiences were incomplete, that there was more work to do to take me full circle. The coyote, the trickster or clown figure for the Native American, was challenging me to not take myself so seriously and to laugh at myself. Unlike my eagle/panther series of experiences that ended with me as the panther "being above it all," this earlier series of experiences did not end with the transformative experience of me laughing at myself. A month later, when I returned to the institute to be part of the Teacher's Training Workshop, I had another encounter with the coyote, this time using the Calling the Spirits posture. This figure from the Olmec era was found in La Venta, Mexico. The posture is usually done as an invitation to those in the world of the spirits, asking them to join us in our ritual space.

My experience using this posture took me back to my spirit guides, the coyote and the bear, now joined by a honeybee.

Calling the Spirits Posture

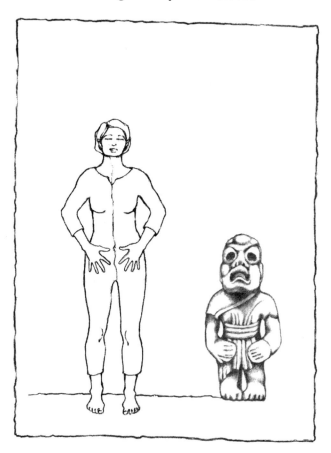

Stand with your feet parallel, about six inches apart, with your toes pointing directly ahead. Keep your knees slightly bent. Position your widely spread fingers on your lower abdomen, with the middle finger of each hand in the crease where your leg joins your torso and your fingers lying against your body. Hold your upper arms firm and away from your body, out to the sides. Eyes are closed and your head is tipped slightly back. Keep your mouth open as though you are calling out, but make no sound.

10-6-10: A bee was caught in the flow of air of my breath. It asked me to hold my breath for a moment so that it could escape and bring me the spirit I was calling. I did, and it left, soon to come back followed by a bear. The bear wanted me to feed it by gathering some honey. As a beekeeper who has successfully kept bears from my hives, this placed me in a dilemma. My coyote was standing to one side laughing. Though the bear was not outwardly laughing, inside he was laughing: he had put me on the spot and I felt it. Though the bear was nurturing and strong, I still gave him electric shocks instead of honey.

As a beekeeper I have an electric fence around my hives to keep out the bears, but an electric fence is not sufficient because the bear does not feel the shock through its coat of fur. To stop the bear I have to hang pieces of bacon on the electric fencing so that when the bear attempts to bite at the bacon it will experience the electric shock on its mouth. I imagine this is where this imagery came from.

This experience demonstrated to me that there was, as I expected, more to be accomplished in my journey with my coyote spirit guide. The coyote and the bear were still laughing at me, and I felt myself in a bind, unable to laugh at myself, caught between protecting the bee and feeding the bear.

Back home, I had to wait about three months to get an answer. It came in the form of the previously mentioned experience in which I shape-shifted into a black panther using the Olmec Prince shape-shifting posture and felt I had finally cultivated the attitude of being above it all—the attitude the eagle had been trying to show me. I had learned how to "rise above" my problems. Once I resolved this issue, I was able to return to the coyote, and in a sequence of journeys, I began to understand his message. For this next journey I used the Jama-Coaque Diviner.

1-27-11: I went through my list of past power animals, but the one that was determined to get my attention was the coyote. He kept popping up between and among my thoughts of the other animals. Then he just sat on his haunches looking at me cross-eyed, with his tongue hanging long as if he thought I was crazy. He reminded me of a drawing I have seen of a coyote—sort of Picasso-esque. He was telling me to not take this stuff so seriously—the Heyoehkah. I was just pouring with sweat. The resolution of some problem, very vague, is to not take things so seriously.

Following this experience, I used the Jivaro South American Lower World posture.

2-3-11: The coyote ran excitedly to me and then ran away, over and over, trying to get me to follow it. I followed. At times he limped, making fun of my slowness. He ran to what we've named at home Coyote Canyon and under the brush in the canyon. I had to get down and crawl under it to follow. He ran up the other side and up the mountain, playing with me to follow, testing me. He ran into the rocks, into a cave where he just sat looking at me like he did last week in that crazy way, telling me I am crazy—challenging me physically, getting me to laugh at myself.

Coyote Canyon is a ravine the other side of our garden where we throw our meat scraps and other carrion and where I did see a coyote a couple of summers ago.

A few days later I went into the underworld using the Sami Lower World posture.

2-6-11: I went to the cave below the railroad tunnel with the four like-minded men I have been with before. They were telling stories of the coyote when a coyote happened to wander in. It looked at me with its crazy look and turned to leave. I automatically followed it, and it led me home. I became the coyote and went in, though my wife did not see me as a coyote in her kitchen. I sense that she felt impatient with my interruption, but instead of reacting in my own impatient manner, as usual, I just looked at her in the crazy coyote manner.

The coyote had told me repeatedly to not take myself so seriously, to laugh at myself and at my physical limitations, and now to laugh instead of having a knee-jerk reaction when I feel my wife's impatience. Letting go of my reactivity to her is my greatest challenge, a lesson the coyote had been trying to teach me.

The following week I had the opportunity to practice my coyote sense of humor when in another group we happened to use the Jama-Coaque Metamorphosis posture.

2-17-11: The coyote is sitting in front of me. He then rocks back on his butt in the Jama-Coaque posture, throws his head back, laughing. After a few minutes he comes to me, licks my face, and takes the sleeve of my shirt in his mouth and pulls. I get up on all fours as a coyote and follow him to his den. Several pups come out and start jumping all over him. He is laughing in joy, and then the mother coyote comes out and looks at him in disgust. The father continues playing and ignores her. She eventually goes off to find them dinner. I then leave as a coyote and head home. On the way I catch a rabbit for our dinner. When I get to the door, I lay the rabbit on the doorstep and start howling. Toni comes to the door, finds the dead rabbit on the step, and calls me in disgust. I return to my human self and dispose of the dead rabbit by taking it to Coyote Canyon, and this time I am able to laugh at Toni's disgust.

This sequence of thirteen experiences extended over a period from 5-23-08 to 2-17-09, and it brought me to a new level of realization; I feel that I am now able to laugh at myself and at my reactions to Toni. I have become the clown coyote. I now find greater contentment in my ability to rise above what used to annoy me, and I am able to laugh at myself. I believe these experiences affect me at the mental, physical, emotional, and spiritual levels, the four directions of the Medicine Wheel. Mentally, I have greater understanding of what has been bothering me; physically, I believe that what has been eating at me, my cancer, has diminished; emotionally, I feel more content and am able to laugh;

and spiritually, I am more able to rise above what irritates me and find peace.

In considering the sequences of postures, initially I repeatedly returned to the Olmec Prince, a shape-shifting posture, because I felt there was much the eagle had to teach me. Then I met Ki Salmen who took me on a soul-retrieval journey. She introduced me to the importance a sequence of postures can have, specifically the divination-underworld-transformation sequence. Though I felt something important had happened as a result of the first time I used this sequence, I did not understand or have the words to describe what, so I continued on this journey by repeating the the Jama-Coaque Diviner, Jivaro, Sami, and Jama-Coaque Metamorphosis postures, going into the Lower World twice with the Jivaro and Sami postures. With these experiences I felt I reached a conclusion and with greater understanding than I would have gained from any posture alone. Going into the underworld twice in this sequence, with the Jivaro and Sami postures, likely added greater depth to my search for the unconscious source of my problem.

PART THREE

Extrasensory Connections through Ecstatic Trance

Native Tribes seem able to communicate beyond the range of eye and ear. . . . The mind of one person appears able to act on the brain and body of another. This faculty, known to traditional people, is verified today in controlled experiments and forms the basis of a new branch of medicine known as telesomatic or nonlocal medicine.

ERVIN LASZLO,
SCIENCE AND THE AKASHIC FIELD

11
Cultivating Parapsychological Abilities

Extrasensory perception (ESP), a term coined in the 1930s and popularized by the cognitive and humanistic psychology movements of the '60s, involves the reception of information not gained through the recognized physical senses but sensed with the mind. This term encompasses a wide variety of experiences, from astral projection to out-of-body experiences. Certainly much of what we do in our ecstatic trance posture work fits this definition. However, there are experiences even in ecstatic trance that take us far beyond our ordinary perceptions into the extraordinary. Such extrasensory connections are frequently available to many of us who do ecstatic posture work regularly; these may include contact with the deceased, distant ancestors, and past lives. Mutual experiences that can be described as telepathic in nature also fit into this category.

The postures that have been most conducive to these kinds of extrasensory interactions are the Chiltan Spirits, the Jivaro Lower World, the Priestess of Malta, and the Mayan Oracle; in addition, I have found that the Hallstatt Warrior is very effective for reaching out to ancestors. The Singing Shaman and the Bird Woman of Egypt have also been effective in inducing telepathic states. Though these postures have produced the extrasensory experiences that follow, I believe that almost any posture will work well provided the journeyer holds the intention to do so. And even if one does not establish that as one's intent beforehand, such contact may occur spontaneously.

HEALING FAMILY DYNAMICS
BY COMMUNING WITH THE DEAD

Having an ecstatic experience involving someone recently deceased, whether parent, child, or sibling, can often provide reassurance to the one still alive; as well, such an experience sometimes offers an opportunity for resolution or completion of some issue that allows one to heal some aspect of the relationship. Though some psychologists are likely to explain these experiences as coming from the unconscious mind, there are those who believe that such communication with the dead is quite real, and that the deceased do indeed have a way of "returning" and communicating to those still alive.

Though I have had occasional experiences of visits with my deceased parents, my experiences in visiting my ancient Nordic ancestors have been exceptionally powerful and have led me to greater understanding of my heritage. These experiences have also provided me with a new understanding of the transition from the ancient matriarchal society of worshipping the great mother goddess, through the many patriarchal centuries of violence and aggression, to now the beginning of or return to a more peaceful society that once again respects and loves the Great Mother Earth. These experiences will be examined in the next section of this chapter.

Sarah's husband died six years earlier, and since then she has raised her daughter as a single parent. This daughter has just left for college, and Sarah was feeling the pain of empty-nest syndrome. Using the Chiltan Spirits, a healing posture, she soon found herself on a beach . . .

10-29-07: I was in the scene, holding a baby. Next thing I knew I was underwater, but not alarmed. There was a lot of seaweed and fish. Suddenly, the baby swam away rapidly. In the distance a form approached me that turned out to be my mother. She said, "Don't be alarmed, when you swam away, it was much faster than that." Then it got dark and cold, and I lay down on the bottom in the sand. I realized I was sinking into the sand and looking up like a flounder at the activity of the sea creatures, kelp, and seaweed. I started sinking through the sand down into caves, where it was very hot and stank of sulfur. There were phosphorescent creatures and I felt very uneasy. There was also a strange blue neon glow.

This bridge across the two generations offered Sarah some insight and relief, though the guilt of having hurt her mother with her own departure is seen in her experience of floundering in the sand and sinking into a hell-like cave. Sarah was reminded or learned from this experience that her mother survived the emptying of the nest and she will too. Underwater is an unlikely place for meeting the deceased, but going underwater is a common avenue into the unconscious. Psychologically, Sarah likely knew all of this on a deeper level, and so this experience probably came from her unconscious mind.

Sarah had five more ecstatic experiences related to her relationship with her deceased adoptive parents, experiences that occurred early in our work with the ecstatic postures so were spontaneous and not entered with specific voiced intent, though again unconscious intent can be assumed to be present. And on one occasion, Sarah had a spontaneous "waking dream" that revealed her birth mother to her, a person whom she otherwise knew nothing about. These experiences and also the mutual experiences reported below show Sarah's exceptional sensitivity to the extrasensory. Her concern, in this next experience, was her relationship with her father. Specifically, he had wanted a son and had treated Sarah like a boy; that was okay during her younger tomboy years, but as she matured into a young woman her father's deep-seated desire caused conflict in their relationship.

Using the Hallstatt Warrior, Sarah had an interaction with her deceased father. In this journey, she started out in a beautiful, fragrant rose garden, in which the theme of disintegration that happens with the Hallstatt Warrior was reflected in the roses with huge thorns losing their petals; the garden walkway led to a steep drop-off at the edge of a canyon, where she saw her father below, suggesting the desolation characteristic of the Realm of the Dead.

> *3-31-08: I was in a formal British rose garden. The fragrance was heavenly, but the thorns on the bushes were huge. The roses were blooming rapidly like time-lapse photography and then the petals would drop off as hips appeared and turned into eyeballs. Bricks started dropping out of the sky and when they landed they would creep into position forming a path! I walked the path until it ended abruptly at a drop off canyon of many many feet. My father was at the bottom urging me to jump. "I'll catch you," he cried, but I knew if I landed on him I would probably just kill him. He kept insisting and getting angrier, so I wrapped my arms around myself and walked off the edge with eyes closed. Instead of falling like a stone, I descended slowly. I opened my eyes and looked down. Everything had dissolved into darkness. I panicked and felt my body grow hard and started to fall fast. I made myself calm down and the descent slowed. I made myself relax more and floated, and then started to rise upward. My body started to come apart until there was only my pelvic area floating in space. Then a tiny being that looked like an alien came out of my birth canal. I was confused as to whether to love it or be repulsed by it.*

Though Sarah did not trust the safety of jumping into the pit, when she eventually did, she discovered that she had control by relaxing, and could relax to the point that she started to float upward. At the end, her body did come apart. The experience ended with the birth of a new but alien life, yet she was confused, not knowing whether to love it or be repulsed by it—a new life that she will need to get used to and integrate into a new image of herself, a new guilt free life of having control over her feelings in her relationship with her father. Again her experience beautifully matched the intent of the Hallstatt Warrior posture, with the disintegrating formal garden, going into the pit, and the rebirth as she realizes that by calming down she can rise out of the pit.

Nearly three years after that experience, I touched base with Sarah again about it and asked her if she had any further insight into that journey. She reported that her father did a lot of yelling and screaming when she was growing up, and consequently she would zip her mouth, but eventually, as an adult, she confronted him and expressed her feelings of anger to him just before he died. She has sometimes wondered if that was the right thing to do and was confused because she feared she might have hurt him.

I suggested that as she blossomed into young womanhood—as symbolized by the fragrant rose garden in which that experience started out— this caused a chasm between her and her father, in the form of a canyon in the trance experience. Her father wanted her to have the nerve and trust of a son and jump. When she finally jumped, she realized that she did have control and could descend slowly and even float upward by relaxing. But this made him angry, and she reacted by going into panic, but then realized that panic would cause her to fall on top of him and probably kill him. So she let herself rise up by relaxing, but then she realized that she was coming apart and felt confused about whether to love or be repulsed by the alien life-form that came out of her birth canal—which was what her father wanted of her, to be a boy, which felt alien to her.

I shared this interpretation with Sarah, and thought it valid; while Sarah did too, she saw her experience a little differently. "My interpretation is more focused on the final act of telling my father off for the first time ever, and the fact that he died before we were able to reconnect, with the possibility that the power of my emotional release actually did kill him. The rose garden metaphor in the trance was perfect: he provided a heavenly [in the form of the rose fragrance in the trance] place for me, but he was full of thorns. The alien I gave birth to was the foreign feeling of not being a total person around my father. It is as if I was gay and came out. But I hated that I hurt him so badly at the same time. He really blew up at me the following morning, and now I just wish I had kept silent."

The following year Sarah used the Jivaro South American Lower World posture for traveling into the underworld. This time she encountered her mother and, once again, her feelings over the way her father had related to her as a child.

4-13-09: Suddenly I was sucked away into a tube. I thought I had been vacuumed up by a vacuum hose, so I tried to wiggle my way out. I finally oozed my way out of the tube and saw an elephant. I had been sucked up into his trunk. Just then an alarm clock went off, and my Mom called me to get up for school. I got out of bed and walked down the hall past the guest room, and this teenage boy was in the guest room. My mom said to tell my brother to hurry up. I came downstairs all confused. My mom said that my brother would drive me to school, and I said, "But mom, I don't have a brother." She looked at me like I was nuts and told me to stop kidding around. I said I wanted to walk to school and so off I went. I walked and walked, and things did not look familiar. It started getting dark, and I figured that it was no use getting to school at night, so I turned around and started walking home.

Sarah offered this interpretation of her experience, which provided insight into the dynamics of her parents' relationship not only with her, but with each other: "Of course, when you are adopted, you always wonder if there are siblings . . . I have always thought of not having blood relations as liberating; it has allowed me to collect my own 'family' of friends, which I have done and continue to do . . . I was my Dad's 'son' . . . When I was a kid, the good times were always us doing guy things. Once I hit the age where I no longer enjoyed being a tomboy and turned to girl things, like hair and fashion and boys, we had big problems. On one level I can see my mother's insistence in the trance experience on my having a brother as her wish to avoid all those difficult years with my father. I know she felt badly about not being able to help me much with my Dad issues. She was also responsible for him not having a son, as she was unwilling to adopt another child after seeing how he related to me."

In the following ecstatic trance experience, which occurred one month later using the Mayan Oracle, Sarah gained new insight into her parents' relationship with each other, while at the same time, on a deeper level, she was able to connect that insight to her memory of her relationship with her now-deceased husband.

5-4-09: I started out by consciously thinking of ancient shamans and trying to call on them to assist me on a journey. I wanted to ask if they would communicate with me and guide me. Then I became very aware of the bones in my face and my skull. I saw myself lying in a shallow grave, and I arose as a skeleton. There was another skeleton waiting for me, and many others around. The setting was a fern-covered woods. We followed a path. There were indigo balls of light puffing out here and there in a weird, pulsing way. We came to a clearing, and there was a huge blue ball that was opalescent, like a pearl sitting on a stump that had been ornately carved. This ball began to spin and looked like the proverbial crystal ball, with indistinguishable images all swirling around inside it. Then smoke arose from it, and colors looked like they were projected onto it. I became aware slowly of the holographic image of a bride and groom at their wedding ceremony. Then I realized it was a very young version of my mom and dad. They looked so young and happy, full of hope and promise. I realized I had never seen them that way. Then my flesh and skin came back.

Sarah reported that the month of May had always been difficult for her because that was the month that her husband had died of cancer now eight years prior, as expressed in the desolate scene and the presence of bones. However, she said this trance experience had been a healing one: "This past May was the first one that lightened up for me, and it may have had something to do with this journey. Dwelling on death for the whole month of May each year, up until the anniversary of his death on the 30th, was routine for me. Many of these journeys have a cleansing influence. I have had a difficult time remembering the great times we had together because of the horrific way his life ended and the fact it ended so soon, leaving me with a career I could no longer carry on alone and a twelve-year-old to raise alone. Life got really hard for me after he passed away, having no family for support. But I give credit to my daughter for actually saving me from a lot of depression and bad times because she gave meaning to my life. I have only just this past year started to feel the shift, from horror, frustration, and sadness, to remembering the good times together. I see the vision of my parents looking so happy and full of promise as a reminder that I need not choose to look at the part of my own marriage that makes me feel bad. I know they would want me to concentrate on the positive, and I think that is why I saw them in that light and not in their usual ho-hum relationship."

The following January, our weekly group took an ecstatic journey specifically with the intent of communicating with ancestors, using the Hallstatt Warrior posture. Once again, Sarah's experience, as we will see in her waking dream from after this experience, was relevant to her relationships with her parents, in this case her birth mother, whom she knows nothing about.

1-17-10: I was standing in front of a fire in a dark cave, when a tentacle or vine came from above and wrapped around me. Then it started to raise me up through a vertical tunnel of bones. The bones looked human and old and were separated in layers like rock would be, with all one kind of bone in each layer, i.e. a layer of femurs, a layer of skulls, a layer of pelvic bones, etc. The tentacle was slowly drawing me up through these bones. It made me think of the catacombs in Rome. I reached the top of the tunnel or volcano and came to an opening just big enough for the vine to pull me through and encountered a blinding ball of white light. Out of this light two huge arms protruded and freed me from the vine, lifting me up above it, where I could see and feel the warm light below me. I noticed an architectural structure that looked like an aqueduct in space. I heard a distant rumbling that grew louder and louder until a huge metal ball came speeding past on the aqueduct, then a second and a third. These balls just launched from the chute into space and disappeared. Then a fourth ball stopped in front of me like it had an awareness of my presence and cracked open. Out came the tentacle/vine and wrapped around me and slowly lowered me back through the volcano into the middle of the fire. I was sad, but then I noticed something hopping around on the other side of the fire, and it was a crow pushing something around on the ground. It was a beautiful pink pearl. I took it and was happy.

Sarah said that this experience was influenced by the eerie sound of Michael Harner's solo drumming on the CD that we used in that session. Her interpretation was that she was experiencing something that she wasn't ready for and so was sent back down. When I questioned her by e-mail the following month, she recalled, "The volcano might have been an announcement or heads-up for the vision of the woman I think to be my birth mother that I had a few weeks later. I had not thought of that, and it had been bugging me as to what I might have been able to see if I hadn't been pulled back into the fire in the middle of the volcano." Then Sarah told me about the waking dream she had a few weeks after the trance experience: "I had an interesting experience on the way home from your place on Sunday. I was thinking about what you said about the possibility of the priestess being my birth mother, and an image of a very old woman popped into my mind. She was sitting at an old wooden table. The whole image brought on the feel of poverty and isolation. The woman had white straggly hair and broken teeth and was sort of scary looking. She had kind eyes, though. She was talking to me, but I could not hear her. It was in black and white, and had the feel of an old-time silent newsreel. The image had more weight than my usual thoughts— more like a dream or journeying. I have always wanted to thank my birth mother for giving me up and letting me go, because I am sure that I had a much better childhood with my mom and dad than she could have given me. I think that is why this woman appeared to me. I realized too late that she was giving me the opportunity to tell her how I felt, and she was gone before I could respond to her powerful appearance. She'll be back, and I'll be ready for her next time."

Because this waking dream had been preceded by Sarah's journeying experience earlier that week, it likely provided her with the energy for the vision she had while driving home. Such related waking visions and night time dreams become very prevalent among people who do ecstatic posture work. Not long after that, Sarah journeyed to the Middle World with the Priestess of Malta; this lighter and more fun-loving experience that included her mother seems to indicate a resolution.

2-14-10: I was calling out to the priestess to come visit me and something, splat, hit me on my thigh, like a paintball, and ran down my leg. It was blue, about the size of a tennis ball. I tried to pick it up, but it was hot and started pulsing to the drum beat and then grew until it turned into a beautiful dark-skinned woman wearing a lot of gold bling. She was dancing wildly and asked me to dance with her. I did, and she moved close to me, then through me, then back into me, and she stayed inside me. I could feel her dancing in my chest. I was moving in ways I had never moved before and felt like I was made of rubber. Then I felt a solid mass start to form in my chest. It became uncomfortable and I had to stop dancing. I felt ill and fell to my knees. When I looked up, my mom was there, looking sort of transparent, wearing her mink coat, which she slid out of and covered me with. I felt comforted and warm. She smiled and said, "It turns out I have no use for this now," and faded away. I laughed because I got the joke.

When Sarah was young and her mother got the coat, Sarah liked to cuddle against it, but her mother would push her away, not wanting the coat to become soiled. After this experience Sarah reported that she had not thought about that coat for years. "When my mom moved to Florida, she actually gave me that mink coat. I was wildly happy and had it altered to fit me, but I was not really able to wear it. I liked it, and it was really warm, which was important since I lived in rural Upstate New York, where the winters are fierce. That was in the seventies. I have stored it ever since. My subconscious has a way of gently reminding me to revisit events and feelings, especially resentments from the past that I thought were resolved. A quote comes to mind: "You may be done with the past, but the past is not done with you." It is telling me to let it go once and for all. As I do, I feel physically lighter.

In this sequence of ecstatic experiences, Sarah faced her various unresolved issues with her adoptive parents and even with her biological mother. The experiences allowed her to release these issues and obtain a degree of healing; by doing so she has begun to feel physically lighter. This was a great step forward, but I suspect that fully integrating these profound changes will take some time yet.

CONNECTING WITH DISTANT ANCESTORS

How are we able to experience our distant ancestors or our own past lives? Such experiences may come from the universal mind, the world beyond our senses, beyond the ordinary to the extraordinary. Communing with our ancestors and revisiting our past lives is beyond what is available to our normal senses and power of reason, yet is believed to be possible by many. The Institute of Noetic Sciences, founded by the *Apollo 14* astronaut Edgar Mitchell, is working on providing clues as to the reality of such experiences and proposing the ways that such communication occurs—through our inner knowing or intuitive consciousness.[1]

Though connections with recent ancestors are very common, likely because of the emotional energy and unresolved issues that are involved in their deaths, I have had a continued fascination with my more distant and ancient ancestry. Though my known ancestral connections are to Germany, England, and the Netherlands, because of the resonance I feel with Scandinavia, especially Denmark and Southern Sweden, I intuitively know that my ancestry goes back to Demark and the western coast of Southern Sweden. The next three ecstatic experiences opened the door to learning more of this ancestry. With these experiences, and a fourth with my Middle World journey in chapter 8, a whole new exciting world of my ancestral family in historic Denmark, which included what is now the Skane, Halland, and Bohuslan provinces of Sweden, opened to me. I greatly enjoy my continued ecstatic posture work in visiting my distant family, have collected more than forty experiences, and I continue to look forward to more visits.

Visiting my ancestors has something to teach me about who I am and about my roots, but also about the nature of who we are as modern people in a more global sense. The next few ecstatic experiences, and the forty some experiences I have collected beyond the scope of this book, show me a thread of consistency in the role of my ancestors as leaders in the community. It seems that we have never been kings, chieftains, or governors, but we have generally been in a secondary role of leadership as respected elders, such as the ship's drummer or in some narratives as the shaman of the community. At the more global level, I am discovering the origin of the aggressiveness of our current testosterone driven society, an aggressiveness that has not always existed and followed a nurturing matriarchal and estrogen driven society that existed during the hunting and gathering era of antiquity, for Scandinavia, an era that started coming to an end around four thousand years ago. As my understanding of these distant ancestors grows, they give me hope that we are moving towards a new age of nurturance, peace, and appreciation for the Great Mother.

My very first experience in visiting my ancestors was spontaneous and I journeyed using the Hallstatt Warrior posture, a Realm of the Dead posture. I felt this posture specifically assisted me in this journey because this statue is from Germany from the fifth century BCE.

1-17-10: I went back to fifth century BCE in Germany—likely one of my ancestral places of origin. I was in a thatched hall, long and narrow, that was near the entrance of a cave. One man, wearing a bearskin, was with me—not the chieftain but the second or third in command. He told me that we were preparing for a hunt tomorrow morning, and some of the men were drawing in the dirt pictures of animals and drawing spears stuck in them. Others were carving on the end of their spears. He then told me that since I was from the future, I must have some wisdom or knowledge to help in the hunt. I shook my head no, but he was insistent that I was to lead them in tomorrow's hunt. We slept on the dirt floor around the fire, and in the morning I took the men in what felt like a random direction, but we did come to several deer. I motioned for the men, about a dozen of them, to spread out, and we herded the deer over a cliff. They all appreciated me, though I still felt like I did nothing or had no special knowledge.

This experience informed me that I am respected and need to have more faith in myself and my intuition, more faith in general, especially in my belief that in this journey I met an ancestor.

A few weeks later I again went back in time. During a session with the Priestess of Malta, a Middle World posture, I found myself journeying without conscious intent to the places of my more distant ancestors; this vision included my father, who died when I was four years old and who therefore feels distant to me.

2-14-10: I fly to Germany (my mother's side of the family), and then to England (my father's side), then to New York and the Hudson Valley, to Pennsylvania, back to Upstate New York, then through Ohio to California—the route of migration of my father's ancestors. Different scene, and stories of my father, who died when I was four years old, flash through my mind: a picture of him holding me when I was an infant; the pictures in the book of my father that my daughter made for me; pictures that he took on his journeys as a seaman around the world; letters he wrote his parents about the books he was reading; the family picture of him and his parents, all sitting and just reading; and thoughts of the interview I had with Gilbert, my father's cousin and college roommate. We were standing face to face, and I could feel his warmth, and that he was proud of me. I felt tears with these thoughts.

From this experience I became aware of a need to connect more closely with my own son. Our relationship is more intellectual—we have great conversations about the books we are reading and world affairs, but I have not seen him for some time, so I traveled a few months later to spend time with him and his wife.

Then nearly a year later I began to experiment with using these postures with the intent to visit my ancestors. Because of the power of my 1-17-10 experience with the Hallstatt Warrior posture, I used it again. In this case I became my ancient drummer ancestor.

12-16-10: I am the drummer on a Viking ship, beating the cadence for those with oars. We are going along a river off the English Channel in Normandy. We come to a dock and pull in. It is also my job to direct the unloading of the boat. The load seems like mainly animal hides. The chieftain goes ashore to a tavern. A teenage boy comes running to the dock; it is my son, and he tells me that grandfather—my father—is dying and everyone has been waiting for me to get home. I turn the unloading over to someone else, leave to go to our thatched cottage, and go in. Papa is on the bed; he looks at me and reaches out his hand. I hold it and feel it go limp. He dies. I look around the room and see my wife holding rosary beads, and a priest. I feel disgusted and start shaking a rattle to ward off the evil spirits from entering Papa. I knew he would prefer that. It feels like the late 900s or early 1000.

Encouraged by these experiences, a few weeks later I tried to contact my ancestors again, this time with the help of the Priestess of Malta. This time it was around the early 800s, several generations before the last episode. This time I was going up the coast of the North Sea, around Juteland, and down the other side to where it now becomes Germany, an experience reported in chapter 8. In these two experiences, the boat we used was a long boat with about a dozen oarsmen on each side and open to the elements. The land in what is now Denmark gradually rose from the sea; it was relatively flat with very low rolling hills with clearings and wooded areas that surrounded the clearings. In the clearings were often found small huts with thatched roofs.

With my fondness for the Nordic mythology with which I greatly identify, I have wondered if I have roots in Denmark. The only clue I have that would support that hypothesis is that my maternal grandfather's name was Willoughby, a Norman name. The Normans were the descendants of the Danish Vikings that invaded and settled in northern France. This trance experiences seem to confirm that.

Though I am unable to prove that the experiences with my distant ancestors are real or that what was experienced represents what life was like a thousand and more years ago, they do bring me closer to my ancestors in an emotional sense. These experiences bring alive within me what life was like back then. They have shown me, at a deeper personal and emotional level, the evolution of our societies, ancient and recent, offering me the hope that we are moving past the aggression and violence of our current world into a new era that brings us back to our origin, to a world of peace, cooperation, and love for Mother Earth.

EXAMINING ONE'S PAST LIVES

One friend indicated that we travel by blood in connecting with ancestors but with spirits in connecting with past lives. Though in working with hypnosis I have had several clients access past lives and in the following experience Jan uses ecstatic trance to do so, I have not been aware of accessing a past life myself, yet I now wonder if my frequent returns to the pavilion of Jama-Coaque in Ecuador might be of a past life.

I was invited to introduce and demonstrate ecstatic trance to group of three people—Jan, Jan's wife Lois, and Jan's good friend Joe—friends whom I have known for a few years. One of the postures I used in this introduction was the Hallstatt Warrior and the journeyers were blind to the intent of the posture. Jan believes in past lives and spontaneously went to a past life in his experience as a child of Inuit bear hunters with the help of the Hallstatt Warrior posture: Jan reported that the hunters were hunting with spears, arrows, and knives on six-foot poles.

8-23-08: I went to a past life in Alaska, a treed area. I was ten or eleven and found myself alone. A group of fourteen people was hunting bear, and I was communicating with them from the other side of the hill. They found two brown bears, treed and killed one of them. We used the bear for food and fat and hide to make things. At the age of fourteen I was killed on a bear hunt. Lois was my mother. Joe was my brother. My father in Alaska was my father from my current lifetime. I died in 1849.

A year and a half later I asked Jan about what he learned from this experience. He responded, "My first thought was that it was just confirming that we incarnate with pretty much the same people (soul group) many times to try to work out things. I also noted the confirmation that indigenous people can communicate without telephones. I didn't pick up on any life lessons from this session." Nevertheless, learning survival skills has always been very important to Jan, and over the years he has wondered why this is so. This experience of a past life may offer an explanation.

There seem to be a couple of distinctions that might differentiate journeying back to past lives and journeying back to visit ancestors. Past lives seem to occur anywhere, in any culture on the planet, while one's ancestry follows a path across the planet as one progresses through time. Also, as with Jan's experience, the people we meet in past lives are often part of a "soul group" of people who we spend time with in both our past lives and our current life, though the relationships between these people may change. From the beginning of Jan's experience he "knew" it was of a past life. My intuition suggests that the people I have met have been ancestors. The belief in reincarnation suggests that there is unfinished business in one's personal growth that is carried through from past lives to our current life, something I have been sensitive to in my work as a psychologist when a client happens to go back to a past life, yet Jan did not report anything in his experience that he felt was unfinished business. My experiences in Ecuador may have been past life experiences; they did reveal the unfinished business I was working on, of rising above what has been eating at me. I have also found threads of unfinished issues occurring among my ancestors, for example from my above described experience of 12-16-10, my disgust with my wife for holding rosary beads as my father dies, but I don't feel that is related to my experiences with my wife now. Maybe as I continue going back to visit these ancestors, such a connection might be found. What seems clearer to me is more global, such as my disgust of the encroachment of Catholicism on our Viking life.

USING POSTURES TO PROMOTE MUTUAL EXPERIENCES

By mutual experience, I am referring to those instances in which two or more people have amazingly similar simultaneous experiences in ecstatic trance—something that occurs far too often to be dismissed in our posture work. These experiences are telepathic in nature, and they tend to occur when the intention to connect in this way is expressed, as evident in the experiment with a group of students I worked with at the Osher Lifelong Learning Institute (OLLI).

OLLI is an all-volunteer nonprofit organization in our county that provides "mature adults with educational, social, and enrichment opportunities." They had invited me to teach four two-hour sessions of ecstatic journeying. In our fourth session, the class of eight, including myself, divided into four pairs. Each pair was instructed to enter the trance experience with an awareness of his or her partner—an experiment in mental telepathy. Though I had experienced many such mutual experiences in ecstatic posture work spontaneously, this was the first time mutual telepathic experiences were sought with clear intent at the outset. After this session of 2-3-09, in which we used the Feathered Serpent posture, all were amazed at the commonality within the paired experiences.

For example, Ron, who was paired with his wife, Carrie, reported:

My wife and I are walking on the beach and it's a beautiful day. There are lots of seagulls in the air and on the beach. We aren't talking, just walking down the beach holding hands. All of a sudden we are transported to the Keno campground with our two grandsons. We are sitting around the campfire roasting marshmallows and talking about the day's activities. I have a very special feeling of togetherness. We were not looking for other significances in these paired experiences.

In her experience, Carrie complained how tired her hand became.

I got very warm, too warm. I could not keep my right hand in that cupped position. It became very tired. I had to move it opposite—stayed that way, then the other hand position, too. I could not make my hands go back to the original position—visualized splatters of water, some white, some black—"little volcanic holes."

The commonality of Ron and Carrie's experience was Ron holding Carrie's hand and Carrie's hand becoming tired.

A second example is seen in Sonja's experience with Gerry. Sonja reported:

A large gray boulder falls from a canyon and rolls and rolls—rolls down and down before it is stopped by land. It turns into an egg, which cracks open, and out comes a pelican, soaring upward—the pelican turns into an egret, then a blue heron. It flies like mad toward the sun. Beside the sun and blue sky is a sheet of darkness and rain. The bird does not want to enter into the rain.

Gerry's experience:

Bright light and white clouds, very cool breeze in clouds. Swirls of yellow, orange, red, turquoise. Bronze swallowtail. Pleasurable sense of snaking through cloud without clear purpose. See glimpses of blue sky and sea below, but I must stay in the clouds. Fly over bridge in the cloud. See a whirlpool of thick white clouds in the distance.

Both experiences involved flight in a blue sky and a view of a stormy sky—for Sonja a sheet of darkness and rain, and for the other person, thick damp clouds. Both experiences included a bird motif.

Another posture that regularly facilitates mutual ecstatic experiences is the Bird Woman of Egypt, a spirit journeying posture to the Sky World that I now introduce. The Bird Woman of Egypt dates from predynastic Egypt, around 4000 BCE. As with many Sky World postures, the person's experience in this posture can often be one of flying, of seeing birds or becoming a bird. Heat is usually experienced with the Bird Woman. The posture fosters a feeling of power and the flow of energy.

Using this posture without intention, Gerry and I found ourselves being propelled by jet energy—for Gerry, from jets in her feet.

7-19-09: I looked from the mouth of a cave on a cliff into brilliant sunlight. The day quickly turned to night. Waves crashed against the cliff. Below, as night fell, the lights of a town appeared. I wanted to go to the town, so I descended first on a tree to a zip line. My feet became jets pushing me through the air until I floated freely. Instead of a town, I landed on warm bioluminescent water. I swam with fantastic, brilliant creatures, and it was great fun. Seaweed made percussion sounds. When I surfaced, I saw an island. It was Japan. Even though it was in the distance, a Kabuki performance with huge figures was visible. I performed a dance that complemented the Kabuki, and the seaweed made music. I wanted to go to Japan, but I didn't arrive. Physically I was hot from head to toe.

In my experience at the same session with this posture, I too felt jet energy, for me from the gas being pushed out from a bag between my legs.

I got hot very fast and kept getting hotter and hotter. Eventually I found myself flying toward the sun. I felt myself as a comet. As I flew through

Bird Woman of Egypt Sky World Posture

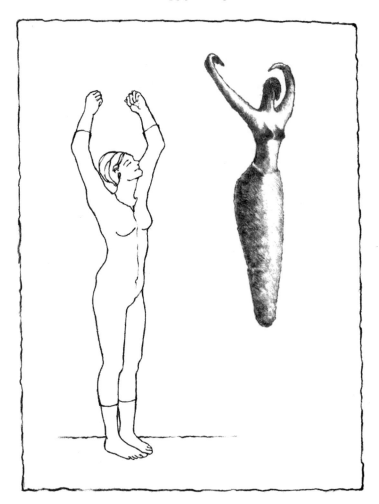

Stand with your feet together and knees locked. Arch your back and fully extend your neck. Make fists with both hands and raise the fists above your head with your arms spread apart as far as they can be held in this position. The knuckles of both fists face each other above your head. Your chin is raised as if to look into the sky, and eyes are closed.

space I felt that my arms encircled a large gas bag and as I pressed against the bag, gas shot out down my legs to my feet, propelling me through space. As I flew I felt a cool breeze begin to cool me. It was very black in space with bright starts shining. At first I could see the brightly shining Earth getting smaller. I was no longer going toward the sun, but out through space.

Note as well that we both saw lights in the distance from a fire in the village or from the stars, and we both got very hot. We were most impressed by the mutuality of these experiences and did not pursue other importance. The mutual nature of these two experiences was spontaneous. We did not enter the experience with the intent of seeking a mutual experience.

In one of our many mutual experiences, Sarah and I used the Singing Shaman, a celebratory posture I introduce here. In general, celebratory postures are simply that: postures used for eliciting a sense of joy or renewal, it is a posture that we might use at the end of a series of experiences to celebrate the experiences of the group.

The Singing Shaman can be found around the world. The oldest image is about 5,000 years old and was found on the Cyclades Islands of Greece. This particular figure is from the nineteenth century, from the northwest coast of North America. In this posture, with the mouth open and the head back, the person in trance often starts to vocalize, making sounds, with a sense of loss of control, or glossolalia.

Without any prior discussion—certainly without any mention of Tarzan—Sarah and I had remarkably similar experiences using this posture. First, Sarah's experience:

1-14-08: I was in the jungle swinging through the trees on huge vines. A man was with me, I think Tarzan, so I figured I was Jane but it turned out I was the monkey. (This posture always cracks me up.) There was a woman swinging with us and we ended up in a tree house where we could all dive off the deck into pools of water that would then "poof" us out and up to vine swings, and we would repeat the process until an angel came, blew

Singing Shaman

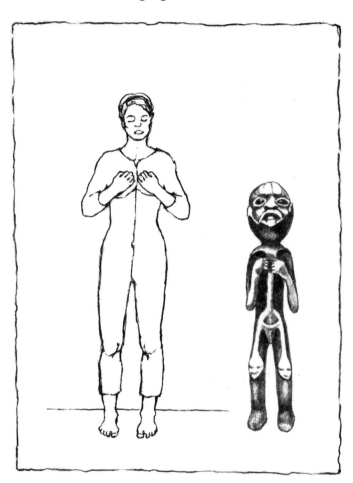

Stand with your feet about six inches apart, parallel and pointing straight ahead. Your knees are slightly bent. Your hands, with fingers rolled slightly inward, are placed on your upper chest, midway along the sternum, with the first joint of each finger touching the chest. Your arms are relaxed and held close to your body. Your eyes are closed, your mouth open and jaw relaxed. Allow sound to come from your throat, but don't force it.

her horn, and made a lot of noise, at which point cranes came and started trumpeting and dancing wildly about. Then it appeared that they were dancing on a piano and making a big ruckus. The piano became a player piano, the cranes slowly faded away, and the piano became an exercise bike ridden by an Uncle Sam character. After a while, smoke started coming out the back like exhaust. This turned blue and filled the room until it was a dense fog. Then appeared something big in the fog, and as it lifted I could see a man on horseback that turned out to be the Shroud of Turin image. He started riding out of the fog but then retreated backward.

I was amazed when I compared this to my experience in this session, though this commonality might be expected, because a common image of Tarzan is of him pounding his chest while he makes the call of the jungle.

I felt like Tarzan, pounding my chest and howling. Then I came wailing out of the jungle into a clearing where the natives were dancing and drumming. I put my head back—mouth open with my fists on my chest—just taking in the drumming. Felt my legs stepping to the drumming, but then I was at an Indian powwow, dancing, strutting in a circle with the other dancers. I had feathers on my arms, swooping, doing the bird dance. I was making sounds, whooping sounds, as I danced. But then I got stuck thinking about the meaning of the bird dance, not knowing what it meant.

Most of both experiences were party like or celebratory, except for the last line in which we both seemed to get stuck, Sarah in the fog and me in my thinking. Again the telepathic commonality was amazing though we did not enter ecstatic trance with mutuality in mind.

Is such commonality a sign of what might be considered mind reading or telepathy? In my experience using clinical hypnosis, as I would lead a client through an imagery exercise, I would often personally experience what the client was experiencing. I believe that this is one important aspect of the power of hypnotic and ecstatic trance: that there is a united field of consciousness between the shaman and the client or patient. The same could be said to be true for two people having a mutual experience while trance journeying with a healing posture, such as what I describe in the next section.

MUTUAL EXPERIENCES FOR PROMOTING HEALING

One of the greatest values of the mutual ecstatic experience is its ability to provide healing energy to the journeyers involved; it also can be very powerful for sending energy to someone at a remote location who is in need of healing. As described in chapter 5, the Couple of Cernavoda posture is often used as a means of providing a mutual healing experience because of the mutual aspect of the posture: there is a female and a male version of the posture, and the male partner intentionally sends energy to the female partner to assist her in healing as she sends the increased healing energy to the person in need of healing, or keeps it to heal herself.

With the intention of exploring our ability to send and receive healing energy as a foursome, Sherry, Faye, Sarah and I decided to use the Couple of Cernavoda posture. I took the male position of the posture while Sherry, Faye, and Sarah all took the female body position. Neither Sherry nor Faye experienced the intense warmth I sent to Sarah, even when I attempted to divide my attention to include Faye. First, my own experience in sending energy:

3-3-08: I felt green vibrations flowing from me to Sarah, a block or rectangle of vibrating energy from my entire body to hers. I felt it was warming her. After about eight minutes, I divided the energy flow to go also to Faye, held that for a while, but the vibrations felt much weaker, so turned them back to Sarah.

Faye and Sherry did not experience the increase in heat as Sarah did, but this might be expected when recognizing Sarah's exceptional ability to pick up such energy as evident in our other mutual experiences. Sarah felt the heat I had experienced sending her.

I got very warm—hotter and hotter—and felt like I was bound and wrapped in black leather and was sweating. The leather was getting tighter and tighter. Suddenly the leather split. I felt like a chrysalis and was cut in half. The (my) inside was all crisp, black, and burnt-out. Ants came and started carrying the pieces away until something like a shooting star came zooming out of the sky and crashed into me. Hundreds of tiny red pieces of what looked like mirrors exploded up into the air, and that was me flying around in hundreds of pieces, making up several shapes—a column, a brick wall, and an arch (architectural). Then I took the form of a fountain with pieces shooting up and out of my shoulders and recollecting in my groin area. It was divine! Then a longhorned steer slowly materialized. It was huge, followed by a rodeo rider on a bucking bronco. I was still in my fountain state so taken by the contrast of calm and frantic. The rodeo rider disappeared into the distance and the longhorned steer got whiter and whiter until it looked like a chalk statue. Then it started rising into the sky and ended up suspended over me. It crumbled onto me (as fountain) and mixed with my red-mirror pieces and slowly I materialized as my human self—feeling renewed and at peace.

I mentioned in chapter 4 that when Lily, the daughter of one of our group members, was diagnosed with lupus, three of us sought to reach out to her with healing energy. Virginia saw a young woman (Lily) riding a white bear, which was ambling through a meadow. The sun was shining and it was playful. At one point the two of them lay down on the ground and the bear cuddled the girl. Later, Virginia observed them flying to a coastal city in Florida. They headed for the beach. The city was white, pastel, with a few tall buildings, a lot of pastel buildings, a white sandy beach and then the blue water. She noted, "In my mind, they are headed for play and Disney World. The image of them is reminiscent of people traveling in a hot air balloon, that is, they seem to float toward the destination, the beach. It is very light out, and it all seems very upbeat, playful."

Sarah's experience was remarkably similar. She, too, was on a beach. When Sarah looked out to the sea, she saw Lily as a little child, swimming. She directed her thoughts to the white bear healer and he appeared up from the ocean underneath Lily, slowly lifting her from the water and cradling her in his arms. The trance went on to include a healing woman and a dolphin, who joined the bear in sending healing energy to the young girl.

Remarkably, my experience also included the healing bear and the motif of water.

Thinking of Lily, I was holding my left hand over my kidney, sending warm energy through my body to the kidney, feeling it on my back. I pictured circular or spiral structures in the kidney that were stiff and straightened. The warmth softened them and let them soften into a spiral. I felt the warmth of arms around me as I was being hugged by the bear cub that I was holding. We were at Lily's high-school graduation party, where I was standing in the backyard. The bear cub wanted to go to Lily, and Lily then was hugging the cub, nurturing it as it warmed her. Its hind legs were wrapped around her, kidney level, healing her as well as feeling nurtured by Lily. It was apparent that Lily needs something to nurture, someone or the bear.

Though lupus often affects a person's kidneys, kidney involvement was not indicated in Lily's diagnosis, yet the kidneys can represent the element of water as was found in the first two experiences, so water might be considered a cleansing element in all three experiences. Remarkably, Lily's condition improved, and no further problems have been reported, even four years later.

WHERE DO THESE EXPERIENCES COME FROM?

The extraordinary experiences that come to us through ecstatic trance can frequently be quite bizarre and at least initially may seem to make little sense; yet upon further examination and with time we find them very powerful. Where do these experiences come from?

At first we may attribute these extraordinary experiences to the unconscious mind, from those deep memories that have simply been forgotten or perhaps repressed because of their painful nature. When such memories come to our consciousness, they often do so in a dramatic, metaphoric language, either because the metaphor is easier to cope with than the direct memory of those past pains or because of some associative process in the human brain, in this case associations that are tied to the forgotten or repressed experience. But the unconscious process cannot account for all that is experienced in ecstatic trance. It cannot account for what appears to be "mind reading," or mental telepathy, which happens frequently in the trance experience. It also cannot account for the divination of future events, another aspect of the trance journey. Before I attempt to explain these phenomena, let's explore more deeply that which is revealed from the unconscious mind and beyond, in our next chapter.

12

Accessing the Universal Mind

According to Jean Gebser,[1] as we continue to move into the fourth era of consciousness, which he calls the integral structure of consciousness, an era of time-free transparency, we will be able to transcend the limits of three-dimensionality. At the same time we will be able to understand and appreciate on a deeper level the power of the first two eras: the era of magic, which is characterized by humankind's intimate association with nature and a kind of dreamlike state; and the era of mythology, in which the separate "I" of the human being emerges, wherein the shaman becomes the conduit of hidden sources of wisdom. These latter eras have provided us with a number of the postures we use in ecstatic posture work, which provide a doorway into time-free transparency. From the era of magic we have our oldest figures, such as the Venus of Galgenberg, from 32,000 years ago, and the Lady of Thessaly, from about 6000 BCE. From the mythic era we can appreciate such postures as the Man of Cuatutla,* from the Quiché Mayan culture, as described in the Popol Vuh; and Tlazolteotl, the Aztec goddess who is still revered by many today.

The idea that we can really appreciate the magical and mythical eras as we move into the fourth era of the integral structure of consciousness is beautifully illustrated by our modern understanding of the myth

---

*A posture not included in this book; the Man of Cuatutla and the Jama-Coaque Metamorphosis postures are essentially the same posture.

of Beowulf, a myth that portrays a journey through the unconscious mind. The story of Beowulf is the story of uncovering and healing the occurrence of an early trauma, the trauma of abandonment.* The pain of early trauma is often repressed because of a child's inability to cope with it. Memory of the early traumatic experience may only arise from the unconscious years later, when the child has grown to such emotional strength that he or she is prepared to face it. In *Beowulf*, Scyld Scefing was abandoned on the shores of Denmark as an infant—the initial trauma—but he grew to become the first king of Denmark. With each successive generation, the power of the Danish king grew, until finally King Hrothgar, Scyld Scefing's great-grandson, became the most powerful king; only he had the strength to face the original trauma of abandonment. The four generations of kings represent the steps in the process of repression and the growth of sufficient strength to face and overcome the torment of the original trauma. With the help of the powerful warrior Beowulf, King Hrothgar is eventually able to conquer his tormentors, Grendel and Grendel's mother. This whole process of overcoming the original trauma is reflected in each line of this epic poem.

Our understanding of the metaphoric language of myth, which comes from the second era of consciousness, demonstrates how we can understand the metaphor of our personal myths, myths that come from our unconscious mind and/or the universal mind, which we can access through our ecstatic trance work.

PHENOMENA FROM BEYOND THE UNCONSCIOUS

In the previous chapter several possible categories of extrasensory experience were considered: communication with the deceased, ancestors, and past lives; and mutual experiences or telepathic communication

---

*This is a subject about which I have written about extensively in *Grendel and His Mother: Healing the Traumas of Childhood Through Dreams, Imagery, and Hypnosis*. In this book I offer a number of case studies of people who have overcome their original trauma by following the process taught us in *Beowulf*.

between two or more people. To this we might add divination experiences, which also appear to come from beyond our ordinary sensory experiences.

These experiences from beyond the unconscious are also found in nighttime dreams, especially lucid dreams. Jean Campbell, in her book *Group Dreaming: Dreams to the Tenth Power*, provides many examples of mutual dreams and of precognitive dreams that predict future events. She points to the many people who dreamt of the catastrophe of 9/11 before the event happened as an example of precognitive dreaming. Robert Waggoner, in his book *Lucid Dreaming: Gateway to the Inner Self*, provides examples of dreams that come from what he believes is something beyond the dreamer—the universal mind. I believe that with time, evidence will prove the reality of the extrasensory qualities of the shamanic ecstatic trance experience. As practitioners enter the ecstatic trance state more frequently, experiences of mutuality, precognition, and communication with the deceased and even with past lives will be attained with greater ease and regularity. The many experiences of the Native American medicine men recorded in Vine Deloria's book *The World We Used to Live In* provide ample evidence for this possibility.

Dean Radin is the laboratory director of the Institute of Noetic Sciences. In his book, *Entangled Minds: Extrasensory Experiences in a Quantum Reality*, Radin clearly shows through the meta-analysis of a broad spectrum of research studies of extrasensory experiences the reality of these experiences. Radin reviewed seven research designs of mental-telepathy experiences, including dream psi, Ganzfeld psi, conscious detection of being stared at, dice psychokenesis, and random-number generation psychokenesis. Each of these experiments demonstrated the presence of extrasensory perception. In performing a meta-analysis of the seven experimental designs combined, of the 1,019 studies demonstrating the presence of psi or "information gained from a distance without the use of the ordinary senses,"[2] the odds against chance were 1.3×10^{104} to 1.

One more example of nonlocal connection is found in the study of telepathic communication between twins. In his book *Twin Telepathy: The Psychic Connection*, Guy Playfair tells about a 1997 television program that is cited by Lazlo.

> The production team tested four pairs of identical twins. The brain waves, blood pressure, and galvanic skin response of the four pairs of twins were rigorously monitored. One of the unsuspecting twins in each pair was subjected to a loud alarm fitted to the back of the chair in which he or she was sitting. In three of the four pairs, the other twin registered the resulting shock, even though he or she was closeted some distance away in a separate and soundproof room.[3]

EVIDENCE FOR THE UNIVERSAL MIND

Two writers whose books I have had the opportunity to review, Ervin Laszlo[4] and Rupert Sheldrake,[5] offer solid theories to explain these occurrences. Both writers start with the basic assumption that there must be a stimulus of some sort that carries the extraordinary information, and there must be a mechanism within a person in trance to receive this information.

Rupert Sheldrake theorizes that since the planets are held together by gravitational fields, fields that influence the whole universe and everything within it; and molecules, atoms, and subatomic particles are held together and influenced by quantum fields; then these fields must play a significant part in holding together and influencing living cells, body organs, living creatures, and everything in the universe. The term he uses to describe these cell, organ, and body fields is *morphic fields;* Sheldrake believes that all memories, everything that has happened in the universe, is saved in the energy structure or waves in these morphic fields. For example, in each of us, our liver's morphic field and our brain's morphic field, along with the fields of every cell and organ of our body, have a memory and communicate with one another to cause our body to work as a unified whole, and the information within these fields has given and gives direction to evolution. Sheldrake suggests that the nerve cells of the brain determine how memories are stored, but storage itself is within the morphic field of the nerve cells.

Sheldrake maintains there is also a field beyond the field that determines each of us, a field that holds together and defines all human beings and other living creatures. He offers as a demonstration of such a field the observation that when a flock of birds moves, it moves instantaneously in unison, without any apparent sensory communication except for the field that holds them together. Another example is the tit, a bird that learned to peck open bottles of milk delivered on doorsteps, a behavior that rapidly spread from one incident in England to other parts of England and across Europe and included a number of different species of tit. Sheldrake suggests that this behavior was passed on to other tits and to future generations of the bird through the morphic field for this behavior.

Ervin Laszlo takes this concept of fields and how they work even further. He calls them Akashic*[6] fields and applies to them the characteristics generalized from particle or quantum physics and cosmic physics. Laszlo recognizes that what we once believed to be the basic building blocks of the universe, the atom and its subatomic particles with mass, is no longer the case. From modern physics, quanta, whether matter or energy waves, are not entirely separate realities, because once they have shared the same state they remain interlinked forever, without the expenditure of energy, no matter how far they may be from one another. These characteristics of quanta define the concept of nonlocal coherence. Another characteristic of quanta is that upon collision of two subatomic particles, some fragments may go backward or forward in time. This characteristic, along with Einstein's theory of the relativity of time, prove that the evolving era of consciousness—Gebser's fourth era—is time-free.

---

*The Sanskrit word *akasha* is "the all-encompassing medium that underlies all things and becomes all things."

The concepts of nonlocal coherence and the relativity of time, when applied to human consciousness, explain the possibility of extrasensory consciousness, including such phenomena as mental telepathy, communicating with the dead, and precognition. Even though at present only a few exceptional people exhibit these powers, Laszlo believes that we are entering an era where we can again cultivate them.[7]

Laszlo describes the Akashic field that allows for such nonlocal communication as a matrix of intersecting waves of energy, holographic in nature. The same way a holographic image is formed through the intersection of laser beams of light, which is a way of storing the information of an image for eternity, the matrix of intersecting waves of energy in the quantum field is the memory that allows for the repeated creation of atoms and more complex molecules; this accounts for the remarkable coherence of the quantum world. In the same way, the Akashic field retains all information and is thus the source of coherent nonlocal communication. The present era's technological equivalent of this is cloud computing, the buzzword du jour. Laszlo calls the formation of stored and recoverable information *in-formation.*

[A] subtle, quasi-instant, non-evanescent and non-energetic connection between things at different locations in space and events at different points in time. Such connections are termed "non-local" in the natural sciences and "transpersonal" in consciousness research. In-formation links things—particles, atoms, molecules, organisms, ecologies, solar systems, entire galaxies, as well as the mind and consciousness associated with some of these things regardless of how far they are from each other and how much time has passed since connections were created between them.[8]

If there does exists a field—a morphic field as proposed by Rupert Sheldrake or an Akashic field as proposed by Ervin Laszlo, both of whom describe what may also be called the universal mind—that unites everything within the universe and is the universal memory of everything that has ever happened and will happen, how do we access this in-formation? It is apparent from examining the powers of traditional shamans and the current use of altered states of conscious that access to the universal mind is attained while in a state of trance. Is there a physiological mechanism that receives this in-formation? Laszlo suggests that the cytoskeletal structure of the brain, the structure that has been thought to provide structural support to the neurons of the brain, is in fact the sensory organ that receives this in-formation.[9] The cytoskeleton is composed of 10^{18} microtubules (compared to the 10^{11} neurons that compose the brain), which comprise a microtubular lattice that could receive in-formation from a lattice or matrix of intersecting waves of energy.

WHAT IS BEHIND THIS EXPERIENCE?

Dream researcher and past president of the International Association for the Study of Dreams, Robert Waggoner (mentioned above), has studied lucid dreams, those dreams within which the dreamer is aware that he or she is dreaming. In his pursuit to understand lucid dreaming, he asked within a lucid dream: "What is behind this dream experience?" or "From where does this dream come?" On several occasions his lucid dreams showed him a blue light that he describes as an experience of pure awareness. In the first of this series of lucid dreams, his dream was simply of a blue light: "There was no action, no objects, no figures, no me, no nothing—just blue light." On another occasion he reported from his dream, "The light is dim, so I shout out to the dream, 'Turn on the lights,' and things became much brighter. At this point, I notice a figure composed of blue light. The figure is about three times larger than I am." The following month he offered the following dream report: "As if a floating point of light in an expanse of aware, living light, the selfless awareness exists. Here all awareness connects. All awareness intersects. All knowledge exists within the brilliant, clear, creamy light of awareness. Awareness is all; one point contains the awareness of all points;

nothing exists apart. Pure awareness, knowing, light . . ."[10] What a vivid description of this holographic matrix of waves of energy!

From Laszlo's collection of Akashic experiences we find another description of this matrix of intersecting waves of energy in an experience described by Alex Grey, a visionary artist: "I felt and saw my interconnectedness with all beings and things in a vast Universal Mind Lattice. Every being and thing in the universe was a fountain and drain of love energy, a cellular node or jewel in a network that linked omnidirectionally without end. All duality of self and other was overcome in this infinite dimension. I felt this was the state beyond birth and death, beyond time: our true nature, which seemed more real than any physical surrounding and more real even than my physical body."[11] Similar visions of a field of lattice-like intersecting waves of energy have been reported in the ecstatic trance experience, as reported by Susan, who used the Jivaro South American Lower World posture.

> *7-1-07: Yellow landscape sand, I see a small child with a red jacket who is part of a tribe (Morocco). The tribe travels in harmony with the ley lines. I am aware that the tribes are responsible for the integrity of the ley lines. The tribes should remain separate to maintain the intended structure of the planet, just as some structures are made of wood so that they are well insulated and some of metal so that they are strong. Marriage between the members of tribes should occur at nodal points so that the qualities necessary for the planet are maintained in sacred balance. Marriage between tribes is okay. There were implications for the natural division of nations, the dharma of the families, within tribes, within clans and within nations. Historically, the travel of the tribes was at the direction of the shaman, who had the understanding of the integrity of the planet and the need to merge with other tribes to balance the movement and emergence on a cosmic basis.*

This experience describes waves of energy that Susan calls "ley lines," lines of harmony and integrity that provide knowledge to the people from their nodal or intersecting points, again, a description of the nature of the universal matrix. In most if not all ecstatic experiences there is a more personal meaning. For Susan, this meaning may have something to do with the balance of diversity and integration in her life, balance and integration that can be learned from the in-formation of the universal mind.

Mike, using the Hallstatt Warrior, a Realm of the Dead posture, experienced undulating, vibrating patterns of energy entering his third eye. He was a vibrating spiral around which flowed two golden, shimmering snakes. He related this spiraling pattern to strands of DNA. The snakes were from the image of the caduceus and were integrating his left and right brain for healing.

Susanne had a very similar experience, also using a Realm of the Dead posture, the Cyclades.

11-27-11: I am a mummy wrapped in muslin. My spirit leaves my body as a snowy white owl. It says "fear nothing." I see huge strands of DNA, vibrating, undulating, intertwining, and moving very fast. The DNA seems like a huge paper Chinese dragon in a parade. I have a strong feeling the DNA is very driven with purpose, that purpose of evolution into higher forms of being. It cannot be stopped. As myself doing the exercise, I am shaking and undulating too. I feel energy intertwining, going up my spine. The owl hugs my mummy self and untwines my wrappings. I dance with the DNA.

Faye, with the Feathered Serpent, experienced the all-knowing part of her soul, merging herself with an incarnate knowledge that would be with her always.

3-24-08: Flying to the sun, moon, into them, beyond, observing life from a distance, soaring high, then into a dark hole, deeper, slithering in the darkness and to a place where I met a part of myself that wasn't here with me: the all-knowing part of my soul. Ask any question. I knew I was running out of time, so I quickly choose healing myself—how to—then a third eye in my stomach, third eye in my heart, third eye in my whole being.

Then merging with myself so the knowledge would be with me always,
merging with my higher self to incarnate this knowledge.

I did not ask the question "From where did my experience come?" until after I read Waggoner's book. Since then I have suggested from time to time that we ask this important question in our trance group. On one occasion, using the Jama-Coaque Diviner to help heal a young girl, I asked the experience where it came from. I then saw a blurred, mesh-like haze of vibrating energy between the girl and me.

> *2-21-10: Again I went to the village in Ecuador to the pavilion of Jama-Coaque. He said that he was expecting me and wanted me to sit with him and that a mother was bringing in her daughter who was in pain. I sat in this posture next to him. The mother came in and sat across from us with her daughter's head in her lap. The girl looked to be in her early teens. We sat in silence—after a while Jama-Coaque reached over and touched my arm, pointed to the girl and indicated by pointing or scanning over his body—that he wanted me to show him where the problem was. I pointed to the left side of my belly and he nodded yes. He went over and put his hand into the girl's belly and pulled out a green glob. [I asked what is behind this experience or where is it coming from?] I stayed there and felt the pain and now the relief of the pain in my own belly. I realized that I got the answer by how I experienced her in myself. I did see a blurred mesh-like haze between me and the girl that was vibrating in energy.*

The question, "From where did the experience come?" was also asked by Greg in his journey with the Jama-Coaque Diviner. Greg experienced seeing something normally unseeable. However, he found the way to see, whether through some instrument or telescopic power inside his energized left side, and what he saw was a field of deep, velvety purple.

2-21-10: My arm and hand feel like I'm holding a mallet, a hammer, a periscope, or instrument for looking inside something, like a doctor's instrument. I see a buff or sand-colored three-dimensional cube, and I am aware of a particular smell, like the warm viscera of an animal. My left eye and the left side of my head feel energized; it is as if I have the power of vision, a telescopic power that lets me magnify small things. Suddenly the beige cube inverts and turns inside out, revealing a field of deep velvet purple. I have a physical sensation of lifting up, as if something is rising into my field of vision. The drumbeat has a sub or harmonic rhythm, a "boom, boom, boom-boom-boom" that is insistent and knowing. This vision seems to be lifting from the left side of my chest, up through my arm and hand, along the left side of my face and resting behind my left eye. It feels muscular and powerful and aware. The drumbeat stops and changes, and I feel my momentum reverse, as if backing out of the posture and returning.

Waggoner's own experiences in asking what is behind the lucid dream has repeatedly seen as blue light.[12] Similarly Judith saw the blue and purple colors of such a pattern in the cosmos using the Feathered Serpent posture.

11-5-07: I had a light show. It was as if there were these awesome colors drawing me out in the cosmos. At first there was a beautiful blue, rather a dark blue, but lit up inside, then it was surrounded by aquamarine, it slowly changed into magentas and purples. I thought it was being drawn into the cosmos—as I thought about it I could say like the Aurora Borealis but when I thought that the colors became all murky and un-bright. I consciously tried not to think, just let go and once more the color show over me only this time it was light yellows, turquoises and pinks. Then the music/drumming stopped and the light show was over.

The reports of trance journeyers describing what seems to be the universal mind go on and on; those quoted here give the reader a sense of a possible universal mind or matrix of in-formation that provides the experiences of mental telepathy, clairvoyance, communication with the dead, and premonitions of coming events. Without the images of a matrix of in-formation of intersecting energy waves offered us by Sheldrake and Laszlo, these elements of the experiences described above would have likely been ignored. Yet such experiences happen with clarity and consistency and cannot be denied. Maybe they do reflect each person's experience of the universal mind. I believe that with further training and experience with such avenues of access as the ecstatic trance experience, we can develop or reclaim the skills and powers of our shaman and medicine men of the past in accessing the universal mind.

Conclusion

Going Beyond

THE SEQUENCE OF STORIES

It has been said that one dream is like a snapshot while a series of dreams is like a movie. Healing and growth are more clearly seen in examining a series of dreams than just one dream. The same applies to ecstatic narratives, but with the additional facilitating factor of using postures with specific intent. When I first began using the ecstatic postures I was excited to see how each posture produced the intended experience; eventually, as the excitement mellowed, I found an even greater excitement in following the ecstatic experiences of specific sequences of postures.

From my years of experience in using hypnosis in the clinical setting, I learned that a beginning point in change is to use hypnotically the language that promotes increased ego strength or self-confidence. An example of this language is, "Each day in every way you will find yourself feeling stronger, with greater energy." The Bear Spirit posture is another way to produce this sense of increased energy and growing strength, the strength of the bear standing behind you, hugging you. Sometimes something, often the feeling of guilt, may inhibit that feeling of increased energy and strength, and you need to be cleansed of that guilt, suggesting the use of the goddess who eats the

filth you bring to her and provides you with the rebirth of your innocence, the goddess Tlazolteotl. With this cleansing, the Bear Spirit
can more effectively facilitate your ego strength. In the group setting,
this energy can be intensified or increased by the male participants
sending additional energy to their female partners using the Couple
of Cernavoda posture.

The next step is to hypnotically uncover that which is inhibiting
your life, for example, depression, anxiety, or obsessive worry. This
list can go on and on. John Watkins, a past president of the American
Society of Clinical Hypnosis, developed a hypnotic technique, called
the "affect bridge," that is most effective in uncovering the source of
this inhibition. The hypnotic language of the affect bridge is, "Go
back through time, carrying with you your (depression, anxiety, or
whatever word best describes your feeling). See where this feeling takes
you." Typically, incidents of abuse, trauma, or other emotional pain
are uncovered that occurred during a person's early years. This same
uncovering can occur using the divination postures by asking such
questions of the oracle as "What is the source of my (depression, anxiety, or feelings of inadequacy)?" The answer to such a question comes
in the language of metaphor and may not initially be understood, but
the answer is available to your unconscious mind. Journeying into the
Lower World with the Sami or the Jivaro South American postures
can also show you what you need to overcome that is inhibiting your
health or growth.

With such knowledge, whether conscious or unconscious, it is time
to experience the death of what is inhibiting your health or growth,
and the rebirth of a new self, free of such inhibition. Initiation postures
such as the Feathered Serpent or the Lady of Thessaly can facilitate such
rebirth. Metamorphosis or shape-shifting postures such as the Olmec
Prince or the Jama-Coaque Metamorphosis postures can provide you
with a spirit guide that will lead you back to health and growth. With
hypnosis, pacing the experiences, knowing when the client/patient is
ready for each step, is very important; with ecstatic posture work, a per-

son's unconscious mind is in control of the process, and the experiences happen when the person is ready for such change.

After I became sensitive to sequencing the postures in this manner, I went back and examined the many experiences I had collected looking for these kinds of sequences, and where I found these sequences I almost invariably found examples of change. In many cases, sometimes up to three years later, I was able to share what I had found that suggested change with the journeyer, and the journeyer in turn was able to explain and validate that change. Many of the experiences that were recognized in hindsight have been described in this book. Two examples are Maria's experience of overcoming her snake phobia and her experience of growth in finding strength in her own independence, and Judith's letting go of grief and guilt by seeing the strength in emotionally detaching from her daughter's dysfunctional behaviors for the sake of her daughter's own personal growth. Sarah's letting go of the guilt she experienced in hurting her father just prior to his death is another example; so is Jen's experience in overcoming her feelings of inadequacy. I now use the sequence of divination, journeying into the underworld, and death-rebirth regularly.

I think the old metaphor of the layers of an onion is most valid in examining one's transformation over time. Change often begins with an understanding or belief that the change is needed, meaningful, and important, but real change may only occur months later when the person's unconscious mind is ready to integrate it. The sequence of postures may need to be repeated several times until real change occurs on a deeper level.

The many layers of the onion became most evident to me when I first found the way to "rise above" or "go with the flow" in my relationship with my wife at the emotional level and overcome what was eating at me physically of with the aid of my spirit guides, the eagle and coyote. The sequence of postures to facilitate this change was repeated many times. Then I needed to be able to laugh at myself to really let go of being hooked into certain reaction patterns, and the coyote became my spirit guide. Though the mouse was a power animal for me twenty years ago, he came back to teach me something new: the importance of being responsible, of providing and protecting. I know that there are more layers to the onion and that the next involves the snake and the world tree as spirit guides. The meaning of these spirit guides is just starting to become clear and has something to do with major changes in my life, though what these changes are is yet to be learned.

Each change brings me, and you, to a new level of health and growth toward becoming a self-actualized person, a more creative person. I believe that this process in personal growth can also take me, and each of us, beyond the common experience to the extraordinary experience of accessing the universal mind, where each of us will find the power of the extrasensory and the time-free experience of the ancient shaman in seeing and hearing from a distance, into the past and into the future.

THE ECSTATIC NARRATIVE

I find very exciting the new field of narrative psychology, a concept that is most relevant to understanding the ecstatic experience. Narrative psychology is the study of how human beings deal with experience by constructing stories and listening to the stories of others. Theodore Sarbin, one of my undergraduate professors, left the field of social psychology in the mid-1970s for narrative psychology because he felt that narrative psychology maintained the uniqueness of the individual, whereas all of the other fields of psychology, in looking for lowest common denominators, fragmented the person.[1] I had him as a professor in the mid 1960s, so I missed this exciting transformation. I have only recently discovered this field in reading and reviewing several books on the narrative approach to psychotherapy, including books by Stanley Krippner[2] and Lewis Mehl-Madrona.[3] Essentially, the approach of narrative psychology, and in particular of Mehl-Madrona's narrative medicine, is to bring alive the uniqueness of people through the stories that they tell about themselves, about their lives, and to honor these stories maintains their uniqueness, unity, and integrity. Using this narrative approach, the client and therapist share stories or narratives. In therapy I would often counter an individual's story that revealed some dysfunction, with a story that offered new insights or help.[4] As reported by Kay Thompson of Milton Erickson, the father of American hypnosis, "He taught by parable, but often it would be years before the story would be recognized for the profound lesson it contained, even though previous to the recognition of Erickson's meaning the idea had been implemented and accepted as the patient's own. Milton knew that the individual does not need to defend against story, that he can listen to them as a child would, wondering and curious . . ."[5]

Who I am is my story. I am storied. Telling our stories is the beginning of therapy. The therapist then helps us uncover and rewrite those stories that are dysfunctional. We generally begin by telling the stories of our everyday life, but the stories that come from our unconscious mind, whether through dream work, guided imagery, or hypnosis, are almost always more revealing in describing who we are. But now we have a new yet ancient way to access these stories from the unconscious: the stories that unfold in our ecstatic posture journeys.

The narrative approach to healing is embraced by Lewis Mehl-Madrona, a Native American psychiatrist who has learned the ways of the physician and psychiatrist of our dominant culture but greatly values the ways of his native elders. In his book *Narrative Medicine: The Use of History and Story in the Healing Process,* he says the stories of the family, community, and culture are essential to the healing process. Mehl-Madrona, whose primary focus is on the Cherokee and Lakota traditions, incorporates Native American storytelling medicine ways in his therapy. In listening to the dysfunctional and painful stories of his patients, he uses stories, many traditional, to help them rewrite their own stories. The stories he shares are metaphoric and often are populated by spirit-guide animals with knowledge for the patient that is healing and leads to personal growth. He recognizes that these stories, with their metaphoric language, are a direct avenue to the unconscious mind.

This is the same way that narratives that come from our ecstatic posture work promote health. They use the same metaphorical language, but they come from within the person's unconscious mind or from the universal mind, that is, the mind beyond. Creating our own unique narratives through ecstatic posture work places us at the center of the narrative psychology movement. Each person has the ability to access for him- or herself what is needed for health and growth.

The stories from the unconscious are in a different language, the language of metaphor, a language that we need to learn to interpret for our own personal growth. Many people do not pay attention to their dreams because they find this language intimidating. Some researchers of dreams consider them just random firings of the neurons of the brain and thus they are meaningless. Yet, when we let ourselves learn this new language and begin to understand our dreams, a whole new world opens to us. The ecstatic narrative is no different. As we have seen in the many examples of ecstatic experiences offered in this book, learning this language and understanding these experiences facilitates healing and growth, opens us to attaining higher levels of self-actualization and creativity, and can take us beyond the ordinary, into a world that many people do not believe in or understand—an extrasensory and time-free world of seeing and hearing from a distance, into the past and into the future.

These extraordinary powers were and are known to the so-called primitive peoples. Vine Deloria, in his last book before his death, *The World We Used to Live In,* collected dozens of such extraordinary stories of the powers of the medicine men. Ervin Laszlo recognized one of these extraordinary powers when he wrote, "So-called primitive peoples have long known of such 'transpersonal' links. . . . Whole clans seem able to remain in touch with each other no matter where their members roamed."[6]

THE COMMUNITY EXPERIENCE

Lewis Mehl-Madrona believes that healing and personal growth cannot occur apart from the family and the community.[7] I agree and recognize the power of the group experience of a community of believers and supporters. These experiences are most effective in the group setting, where positive energy is increased and shared. The power of the group is much greater than the sum of its parts.

According to dream researcher Kelly Bulkeley, the Senoi, a native people of the Malaysian rain forests, daily share their dreams publicly. Some attribute their idyllic, nearly conflict-free community life to this practice.[8] My dream is that within our community we will begin to value and see the value of dream groups and of ecstatic-trance groups. I hope that soon my schedule will allow me to spend time several mornings a week at our local coffee shop, making myself available to facilitate a dream group. The setting, with its couches that sit in front of a large stone fireplace, is idyllic. Within the homes of our community, ecstatic-posture groups will continue as they have for the last five years, but I hope that they will grow and continue to expand into other communities throughout the country just as they expanded to other communities near my home.

We as a people need to come together and relate, not just in the everyday world, but also in the world of the unconscious and in a world that can access the universal mind. Then we will move toward greater health and creativity, finding again the power of the ancient world through our ability to access the extraordinary. This will be a world where each of us will again know the power of the ancient shaman.

Appendix A

The Healing Powers of the Native American Medicine Wheel*

Atop Wyoming's Big Horn Mountains is an elaborate configuration of stones. These stones lie in a pattern resembling a large twenty-eight-spoke wheel, eighty feet across. It is estimated that perhaps five million similar stone circles or medicine wheels, from five to thirty feet in diameter, existed across North America. Artifacts found at the Majorville wheel in Alberta, Canada, indicate the age of this medicine wheel is from 4,000 to 5,000 years old, built at the time of the construction of the Egyptian pyramids. Eddy described these, and other medicine wheels, many from 100 to 200 feet across. His evidence suggests that these wheels were used as calendars and instruments of astronomy.[1] Anthropologists might attach a religious significance to such artifacts as the medicine wheel and the medicine bundle, believing these places and objects were used in the worship of the sun, stars, or moon.

Native American literature and "teaching tales" suggest that neither the astronomical nor religious significance seem adequate in describing the significance of the medicine wheel. The medicine wheel functions more centrally in life and provides a framework for growth and direc-

*Written by Nicholas E. Brink. Originally published in *Imagery: Current Perspectives,* 45–54. Edited by Joseph E. Shorr, Pennee Robin, Jack A. Connella, and Milton Wolpin.

tion in one's life. The medicine wheel has implications for psychology and psychotherapy.

THE MEDICINE WHEEL

The medicine wheel is a concept and life process among the Native American, providing the individual with emotional and healing strength and direction to life. In a concrete form, the wheel is symbolized by the four directions, most concretely, as rocks on the ground designating the four directions, but also found in other symbols, shields, medicine bundles and ceremonies. Each direction is represented by an animal, a color and personal characteristics. The medicine wheel is personal to each individual and its meaning is fluid and different from individual to individual. For example, the medicine wheel of Hyemeyohsts Storm[2] describes East as the color gold, as represented by the Eagle and with the traits of being farsighted, concrete, rational, and action oriented. South is the Mouse, green, and the childlike, trusting, innocent, sexual, and physical side of the individual. West is the Black Bear and is the individual's deeper, darker, introspective, and emotional side. North, the White Buffalo, is wisdom, understanding, strength, and spirituality.

Understanding the characteristics of animals is a very important and beautiful aspect of the medicine wheel, an aspect that is not well understood or used by this writer because of his limited involvement with animals. This paper presents the more personal use of the medicine wheel to this writer as a psychologist.

The Medicine Wheel, in the abstract sense, is life and a truth greater than life, yet it is different for every individual. It is recognized as real, yet evasive, and difficult to define. When a child is born, the child's parents search or wait for a vision that characterizes the child. This vision is described in terms of one of the four directions, and provides a name for the child. A major task in life is then to search the four directions to become a complete person. The process of the search is most important and lifelong, and a specific goal of the search is not assumed or expected. As the four directions are searched, the personal meaning to the individual continually changes.

THE VISION QUEST

For the Native American the search of the four directions is seen as a continual vision quest. This concept was popularized in literature in the book *Lame Deer, Seeker of Visions,* by John Fire Lame Deer and Richard Erdoes.[3] The book begins by describing the vision experience when being "alone on the hilltop." Such a quest is initiated intentionally with no expectations as to what will be seen or found. The unknown is faced with anticipation for discovery and change. What is seen or experienced on such a quest is considered relevant and valuable in one's life. The visions experienced can be referenced to or by the medicine wheel. The visions gained when being totally alone, as when "alone on a hilltop," are considered North or spiritual visions, visions of understanding and wisdom.

Don Juan, the teacher of Carlos Castaneda,[4] speaks of the tonal and the nagual. The "tonal is the organizer of the world . . . The tonal is everything we know." As an individual moves through life, knowledge narrows our expectations and reality. The nagual is the unknown, that which is beyond the tonal, and by facing it, our world can expand. Andrews[5] teaches the value of finding and facing the unknown. Visions on a hilltop are one means of such expansion. The nagual is "where power hovers." The many vision experiences of Castaneda are Don Juan's means to lead Castaneda to grow and use the nagual. Great fear is experienced in such expansion. Dealing with traumatic images is a source for growth and change.[6]

The teaching tales of the Native American frequently have their source in these visions. Brink[7] presented three distinctions between the Native American tale and the Euro-American Judeo-Christian fables and fairy tales.

CHARACTERISTICS
OF THE MEDICINE WHEEL

The medicine wheel concept and process provides important therapeutic or healthy directions. First, the Medicine Wheel provides for continued growth and change throughout life. Second, the Medicine Wheel is a mirror, reflecting who we are, pulling from within us what is most important. Third, as we use the four directions as a mirror, as we begin to think we have an answer, that answer dissolves to become something else. This evasiveness of the Medicine Wheel may be its greatest power, even though this evasiveness may seem to be a weakness to the White Culture. Fourth, the Medicine Wheel has implications for all of life, whether for the individual, for work, play, or sleep. The following is an elaboration of these four characteristics.

The Medicine Wheel Promotes Change

Our European heritage generally assumes the unchangeable nature of adults. Many models of psychology suggest that children grow and change, but adults are resistant to change. One theme frequently expressed in our Christian heritage is that man is born in sin and continually battles evil without the hope of real change in this condition. From many different directions, we are told we cannot change.

In contrast, the Native American is born with the spirit of the community being that change is expected, that life is the continued search of four directions with the goal being continued growth toward completeness. Though the parents provide a child with a description by naming the child as a result of visions at the time of birth, that name is changeable or added to through further visions.

The Medicine Wheel as a Mirror

The reference of the medicine wheel as a mirror has been made in Native American literature.[8] The wheel reflects the individual's characteristics in his or her search of the four directions. The medicine wheel incorporates the dynamic nature of a mirror (as explained in the next section) as different from a photograph. Many of the models of psychology provide reductionistic descriptions of the individual that do not accurately acknowledge the moment-to-moment changes in life. For example, a model may suggest that people may be either introverts or extroverts, ignoring the many occasions in an introvert's life when he or she is an extrovert. Seeing oneself using some psychological models or tests of personality is like trying to shave while looking at a photograph whereas the medicine wheel is like using a mirror.

The Power of the Evasiveness in Meaning

In reading the *Book of the Hopi* by Frank Waters,[9] this writer initially found the Hopi's use of symbols very annoying. Each symbol has a multitude of meanings. From a rational orientation, symbols with more than one meaning are confusing and meaningless. In our rational culture, the color green should not represent death or envy as well as life and growth. Over the years I have learned to appreciate the diversity in the meaning of Native American symbols.

Each direction of the medicine wheel is described in a number of ways. For example, for the medicine wheel of Hyemeyohsts Storm,[10] East is the eagle and embodies the characteristics of the eagle (e.g., farsightedness). East is the sunrise, the beginning and the color gold. East represents the rational, doing or action oriented aspect of life. In the diversity of this description there is an intuitive unity. Yet these descriptors provide flexibility for change from moment to moment when other aspects of the eagle are noted. Storm's South is the mouse and the color is green. South reflects the individual's sexual, physical, or childlike side, including the traits of trust, playfulness, and innocence. Again, there is an intuitive unity in this diversity and the descriptors add greater flexibility to mirroring the individual. When the West and North are added, the dynamic picture in the mirror becomes complete.

The diverse meaning of Native American symbols makes the medicine wheel a dynamic mirror. In attempting to see oneself in this mirror, the image is always changing and elusive. The individual's search leads to finding a personal meaning. For example, the rational and emotional distinction is recognized as a reality, but in facing West, one's emotional side, and searching for an understanding in the emotional, the emotional side dissolves into rational understanding. A phrase used by Roni Tower in her address at the 1987 AASMI Conference, that is, "Man plans and God laughs," illustrates the evasiveness of the North-South or spiritual understanding and physical-innocence dimension. Are the plans of man or the laughter of God the North or the South? A similar phrase revealing the same elusive nature of the North-South dimension is "everything is important but nothing is important."

This laughter of God is also reflected in the Heyoehkah of the Sioux or the Koyemsi (Mudhead) Kachina of the Hopi. These members of the tribe are the Jungian trickster archetype. The Heyoehkah does everything backward, wearing clothing backward and performing many of the spiritual rituals backward. Such backwardness and humor prevent the community from taking any idea too seriously and, thus, promotes flexibility.

At one moment one sees oneself clearly in that mirror, but the next moment life moves on and the mirror shows a different reflection. The multitude of meanings found in dreams, imagery work, and vision quests can be overwhelming, but a clearer expression of real life rather than looking at a photograph.

The Reflection of Life

The medicine wheel reflects an entire life, instantaneous moments in life or any interval in between. The wheel reflects therapy from beginning to end, a single session, or a moment in a session. The pursuit of the medicine wheel begins in the East and moves clockwise. East is dawn, birth, the beginning of a search, or an individual's decision to begin therapy.

Moving South, the physical, trusting, innocent side of life is the stage of life of childhood, of learning to walk and take charge of one's life. South is gaining trust in oneself, trust in the healing powers that come from within, and trust in one's therapist. South gives one the strength to face the West.

West, the dark emotional side of the individual, is the struggle of life, of being responsible to marriage, children, and one's profession. West is getting down to work in therapy, exploring the emotional pains of life, and facing the unknown. Facing these unknowns lead to greater understanding and spiritual growth, the North.

North is the spiritual experience that comes from deep emotional understanding, the peak experience in therapy, or the flash of insight. It is wisdom gained from life's experience. North provides the understanding and wisdom to make the appropriate decision in life, the East, of using the wisdom and understanding to continue in life and begin the circle anew. Each moment in life is reflected on the medicine wheel.

USING THE MEDICINE WHEEL

The Nature of the Journey

Lame Deer's trip to be alone on a hilltop was noted as a spiritual or North vision.[11] The characteristics of each direction suggest the nature of the vision quest.

The journey begins in the East with the decision to seek spiritual understanding. The therapeutic equivalent is the client deciding to initiate therapy.

The journey takes the individual first to the South. The South experience provides the trust and innocence or openness necessary to continue on the journey. For both Lynn Andrews[12] and Michael Harner,[13] this journey took them to a waterfall, and the vision was seen in the daylight in the mist of the waterfall. For Carlos Castaneda,[14] he was instructed to see the world through squinted eyes to intentionally blur his vision. Many of the experiences of childhood provide the source for the South vision. What child has not spun to get dizzy, or seen visions in the clouds? One favorite South experience from my childhood, which continues in my office, is to see things in knots of the knotty pine paneling. The Rorschach cards provide a similar experience. The experience occurs through opening oneself to experiencing the environment in a new manner. The experience requires the individual to perceive in a trusting and innocent manner. The equivalent in therapy is the development of rapport.

With this light, trusting and playful childlike attitude, strength is gained to face the deep, emotional and frequently painful experiences of the West. The West experience is to go down deep in the dark to attain a Vision. Lynn Andrews went deep into a cave.[15] Michael Harner suggests any image of a hole, tunnel or cave.[16] The therapeutic images of going down in an elevator or of going into a cave have generally been considered a means of listening to one's subconscious, of touching deep emotional feelings. Desoille[17] uses the imagery of descending into a body of water. Dreamwork in therapy is another rich source for such East visions. Such East visions provide the emotional energy to continue on with the journey to the North.

The North Vision, the spiritual Vision of wisdom and understanding, is attained through being totally alone. Lynn Andrews was left by her mentor alone in a cabin during the winter in a remote portion of Manitoba for an extended period of time. Lame Deer went to the top of a mountain. In this state of total aloneness and with the emotional energy of the West, and the trusting and innocence of the South, a vision of understanding and wisdom is attained. In therapy, situations of being alone are frequently explored and challenging ones are often prescribed. During the therapy session, experiencing going down in an elevator frequently results in finding emptiness or a void. Exploring that emptiness or void can lead the client to find that which fills the void. When the client identifies an empty or void experience, the "affect bridge" of John Watkins[18] is frequently used to initiate such an imagery journey. John Watkins has the client identify and describe an affect and then instructs the client to carry that feeling while going on such a journey.

The spiritual experience of a North provides the individual with an "act of power," or a decision of what needs to be done upon returning to the East, the place of "doing." The "act of power" then provides the beginning of the continued journey.

The Medicine Bundle and Medicine Shield

Medicine bundles or medicine shields are created to provide the individual with concrete ways of remembering and reviving the visions. The medicine bundle is a leather pouch filled with objects such as stones, feathers, herbs, etc., that provide special meaning or connection to the visions. A medicine shield is a hide stretched over a frame and decorated in ways to recall or revive the experiences of vision quests. Such objects can be very useful in therapy. Clients are instructed to find something to represent a spiritual learning experience, carry that object or place it in some conspicuous place as a constant reminder that awakens feelings of the experience. These objects evoke the vision experience similar to Roberto Assagioli's use of evocative words.[19] Assagioli's Law III is "ideas and images tend to awaken emotions and feelings that correspond to them." Thus, whether an evocative word or an object in a medicine bundle, the feelings and emotions of the vision are awakened.

Among the Native Americans, such Visions are very individual and personal. These visions can also become a central part of the community and a rich source of ritual, as when reenacted by the community, upon direction of Medicine Man. During the fall of the American Indian, between the time of Custer and Wounded Knee, the Indians were looking for strength. One major source of energy was the "Sun Dance," which spread across the plains. This dance began with a vision of one medicine man. Black Elk also had a powerful vision that was frequently reenacted by his tribe to bring this tribe strength.[20] Such reenactment, as with the medicine bundle and medicine shield, is a means of retaining the power of the experience of the vision.

Facing Fear

Visions, generally of the West and North, are initially experienced as very frightening. In the books written by Lynn Andrews and Carlos Castaneda, such frightening experiences were so severe that they would elicit such severe physical reactions as vomiting. One repeated theme in the Native American literature is that power is gained through facing such frightening experiences. In therapy, these experiences identify a "tormentor" and facing the tormentor results in loss of its power and, thus, gaining great strength over it. Typically, individuals enter therapy running from problems, and one goal is to reverse that attempt to escape and to face the tormentor. Visions, again, provide a rich source of situations where the client has the opportunity to face a tormentor.[21] Frequently the medicine person creates such experiences to force the client to face the tormentor. Jay Haley's "Ordeal Therapy" is one source of how such experiences can be used in therapy.[22]

APPLICATIONS IN THERAPY

The Four Directions

Again, the direction of the search for the Native American is to begin in the East and move clockwise. This direction of search is the same for psychotherapy.

A twenty-five-year-old woman came for therapy because of unhappiness in her relationships with men. She complained of feeling distant in these relationships. The decision to seek therapy was an action of the East.

During the first session, imagery was used to attain relaxation. She was asked to turn her mind inward, becoming aware of her body sensations, sensations of tension and sensations of relaxation. Then she was led in imagery on a walk along a mountain path. These exercises were South experiences, physical and trusting experiences, first to increase her awareness of her body, and then a playful trusting exercise of examining what she saw along a mountain path.

During the second session she visualized going down in an elevator and seeing as the doors opened. She was ready to face this emotional and dark experience of the West. Behind one door she faced a void of darkness. The following session she chose to return to that darkness where she saw a faint source of light. She approached the light and found a chute through which she jumped into the light. She found herself flying along a coastline. This experience was very exhilarating. Though she did not know specifically to where she was flying, she sensed that she had a direction. She left the darkness of the West and was on her way to the understanding of the North, with the unspoken sense of a spiritual experience. Conscious understanding was attained when she saw a restaurant on a point jutting out into the water and she saw a car driving in. She landed to meet her mother, father, and music teacher. She wanted to tell them she could fly but she knew she could not. Her father would say "that's nice," discounting the significance of flying to her. Her mother would say "that's impossible," and her music teacher would try to take credit for her ability to fly. This realization returned her to the East with an understanding of her need to find someone who would be understanding.

Facing One's Tormentor

By facing one's tormentor, personal power is gained. Fear of the unknown is one major tormentor in life. Any change is facing, to some degree, the unknown. By facing one's tormentor, one is saying that one is ready to experience the unknown of change.

An obvious tormentor to a person attempting to quit smoking is the craving for a cigarette. Facing this feeling, the individual might discover that his or her mouth is dry or cottony, experience chest tightness, or cold and clammy hands or feet. For each individual this experience is different. As such feelings are faced and experienced fully, the feelings change, diminish or move to a different place within the body. When the individual experiences the evasiveness of such feelings, discovers that the feelings are not as intense or frightening as expected, or that the mind easily wanders away from the feelings, power is gained over these feelings. As other aspects of the addiction are revealed, these aspects, too, are faced in a similar manner. Similarly, facing the physical sensations of Premenstrual Syndrome provides power to reduce the common behavioral responses to these symptoms.

Facing such feelings is working primarily on the East-West axis. Power is found over the emotions of the West, when examined using rationality of the East. Power is also found over rationality of the East when getting in touch with the emotionality of the West. An example is of the client troubled by psychosomatic symptoms of panic and anxiety. Typically, the client with psychosomatic symptoms is an East oriented person not "in touch" with feelings. Whereas Watkins[23] proposes the affect bridge, Araoz[24] speaks of the somatic bridge. Araoz instructs the client to carry the somatic experience on an imagery journey as Watkins asks the client to carry the feelings. In using the imagery of the medicine wheel, the road signs on the East-West bridge are different at either end. At the East end, going West, the bridge is called somatic, and at the West end, going East, it is called affect. For the client with psychosomatic symptoms, he or she is to carry the symptom on the imagery journey to find the affect. By using imagery to uncover the thinking pattern and fear causing the anxiety, power over the anxiety is gained.[25]

One of the most severe tormentors in our times is cancer. There have been numerous examples of how facing the tormentor of cancer has caused tremendous change within the individual. One example of the spontaneous imagery of a patient with benign fibroid tumors but with special relevance to the medicine wheel was presented by Eugenia Pickett.[26] In a personal communication with Eugenia Pickett, she assured this writer that neither she nor the client had any direct knowledge of the medicine wheel. Yet this client produced the following spontaneous image.

> I enter the land of deep sleep from the West, and am dancing in a counter-clockwise direction over the charred earth. In a scooping motion flower springs from the earth and marks the South. I spin

around, moving to the East, and as I do, snow falls over the entire area. Then I move to the North, spread my arms to the heavens and wait . . . a long time. The moon rises and everything is crystalline, purifying the space, preparing it so it can grow green again in the spring. There are bits and pieces of charred wood showing through the snow and it looks like a large grave for many people. In the East I can see the beginning of a new day-glow of morning illuminating the flower of the South. The sky glows red, and there is something I must do before the sun rises. I rake through the snow and ashes, looking for something among the buttons and snaps and broken bits of things. And I find what I am looking for-a moon crystal. It is a crystal from the past, still here, and I put it in my pocket as the sun comes up on a clear blue-white day. The sun melts the snow. Water seeps into the earth, and tender little shoots appear.

She then continues the imagery ending with "I feel like I have everything I need and that I am all right, and that some kind of cleansing process has begun."

This incredible insight into the symbols of the four directions, yet proceeding, first, in the reverse of the usual direction of movement of the medicine wheel, as might be done by a Heyoehkah, to reverse the evil growth or to let go of something in one's life that was felt most important, in order to produce change, is a major goal in therapy to shrink tumors.

Marital Therapy

A major use of the East-West axis is in marital therapy. Lynn Andrews[27] reports her conversation with Zoila, a Mayan Indian medicine woman. This Indian notes that white women generally live in the West, that is, they primarily exhibit their emotional side, and the white male lives in the East, or is primarily rational. This incompleteness provides a clash in marriage that the only direction such a couple can find in common is their physical-sexual side, the South. She notes that the white culture lacks spirituality of the North.

Expanding this description of our white culture, the difference between the white male and female describes the sexual conflict found frequently in marital therapy. A frequent complaint by the wife is that the husband's approach to sex is "wham bam thank you ma'am." In such cases the husband, if he allows himself to express his feelings, recognizes his impatience with the warmth and closeness sought by his wife. When the husband can take time to examine the emotional side, he can learn to appreciate the warmth.

Finding balance on this East-West bridge can provide solutions to such other marital problems as dealing with anger, guilt, fear and perfectionism. Adding the balance of the North-South bridge introduces the important ingredient of humor to overcome the problems caused by these emotions.

SUMMARY

Psychology has spoken of the four dimensions of the individual: the rational, the physical, the emotional, and the spiritual. The medicine wheel expands these four dimensions into a dynamic and meaningful model of mirroring human life and a model that promotes continual growth and change. East represents the rational, problem-solving, and action-oriented dimension, while West is the emotional, creative and spontaneous dimension. South, or the physical, sexual, trusting, and childlike dimension, is opposite the spiritual, knowing, and understanding dimension of the North. Life is to a life-long search of these four directions.

The power over life begins with beginning the search, an action of the East. Gaining trust of one's self is gained in the South. With this trust one is able to face the more fearful experience of the darker, emotional, empty feelings of the West. Facing the West provides the strength to, alone, discover the spiritual dimension. Out of this discovery of the North, one finds an act of power performed in the East and, thus, continues on the journey of the medicine wheel.

Therapeutic experiences of the South include activities to help the individual gain faith and trust in oneself. Playful, supportive, and ego-strengthening exercises frequently using imagery are included in those activities. The activities to assist the individual to face the deep emotions of the West include the use of mental imagery of descending or going down into the earth or water and of facing one's tormentor. Experiences of the North occur when one is totally alone. Using mental imagery or a situation of total aloneness to face the void or emptiness in life is a North experience. Out of such "alone" experiences come decisions of power that greatly affect one's life.

Appendix B

Ten Days in June*

I woke on Saturday, June 10th—as I have done so frequently over the last seven years—wondering why I felt tense, experiencing tightness in my chest. That morning I realized why, but I need to give a brief history before I begin my account of these next ten days.

In my journey to uncover the cause of my own tension I have uncovered at least three layers. First, when I began my private practice as a psychologist I felt insecure because I was taking a chance in resigning from a secure position, and I was not certain of future success. Success did arrive quickly and I believed that with such success the tension should fade. It did not. The second realization came a couple of years later, while talking with another psychologist. I realized that I feared anger. In realizing this fear and recognizing that anger is often an integral part of psychotherapy, I began to use my anxiety during sessions as a signal indicating that anger needs to be dealt with in a direct manner. My anxiety became a normal and appropriate ally in the face of anger. I felt that this approach greatly increased my effectiveness as a therapist and my life in general. But the anxiety in the morning continued. A third realization was the feeling of responsibility, being responsible to help the lives of others. I have struggled with that idea, and it has led to acceptance but no great change.

---

*Written by Nicholas E. Brink. Originally published in *Imagination, Cognition and Personality* 11, no. 1 (1991–1992): 99–102.

213

My most recent realization came that Saturday morning.

While still in bed, I realized that I have not trusted people for most of my life, even though, in both my conscious belief and in my behavior, I do trust people. Such remembrances as the fact that I was usually chosen last for the kick-ball teams in elementary school, that I was dyslexic and initially did not do well in school, that I was socially backward and did not date until college are just a few of the precursors of my long-lasting feelings of insecurity and fear of being hurt by others. I had a fear of using the telephone and was afraid of talking with people who I saw as authorities. As is apparent by my success, I have been a person who has always faced these tormentors. I was dyslexic but eventually earned my Ph.D. My social backwardness was outwardly overcome by becoming a successful psychologist. For about six months, a number of years ago, I worked in the complaint department of a large department store to overcome my fear of using the telephone. I never did become a successful athlete, but I overcompensated in other areas. On the surface, I should not have been troubled with this anxiety over the years.

The realization that my anxiety was caused by these deeper feelings of lack of trust and fear of being hurt by others was not enough to allow me to wake up in the morning feeling rested and quiet inside. From my experience in using hypnosis and mental imagery to help others with anxiety I do understand why. I know to change such subconscious beliefs takes "talking with" the subconscious mind through dreams or image work. Psychologist Daniel Araoz[1] in translating psychoanalyst Charles Baudouin[2] of the new Nancy School* in France states as his first law: "it is not willpower that produces change but imagination." I had changed my behavior through willpower, but in my imagination I was still the hurt and untrusting kid. I spent much time over the next ten days using relaxation techniques and attempting to open my mind to wait for the needed images. In some ways I was trying too hard.

---

* The Nancy School was an early French school of psychotherapy founded in 1866. It was based on psychology and verbal suggestion using light hypnosis with no amnesia effect.

During these sessions of meditation I would intentionally recall those incidents of the past and then attempt to lay them to rest with thoughts of how I have overcome those tormentors.

It so happened that on Thursday, June 14, I was to go to a four-day meeting of the Third World Conference on Imagery. On Sunday, I was to present a workshop on power struggles. This conference gave me the time off, a forum to work on this struggle within myself, and a place to share myself with a number of beautiful people at the conference who did not know what they were doing for me. Their ability to listen and, especially their humor, was what I needed. I spent a good hour or more each evening in my room meditating on these beliefs and waiting for the necessary imagery. When finally the imagery came, I was not ready to recognize it for what it was until my four-hour trip home Sunday evening. On Saturday afternoon I went to a workshop on animal imagery and met several animals with the help of Rene Pelley a-Kouri. I frequently use animals in therapy with others, but I use animals in a different manner. I found Rene's model interesting. I use a model of the four directions of the medicine wheel to provide structure to the imagery of animals,[3] while Rene used the seven chakras.[4] It was the merger of these two models that caused the confusion that delayed my understanding, but it was just that confusion that I needed to break me away from trying too hard. Rene first asked me (and the whole group) to allow an animal to come out of my heart chakra. My image was slow to form, and only when drifting off into a deeper trance, in which I saw a modern ranch-style house with a sloping driveway and a new car in the driveway (no house, driveway, or car I have known) did my imagery become spontaneous. I was washing that car and a few feet away on a tall tree was a squirrel with its tail darting back and forth, asking me to follow it up the tree. I stood there wondering what the squirrel was all about.

The second image was from my third-eye chakra and again it was slow in coming. I waited to let go of control and that control was eased when I began to float through a black tunnel that opened onto a very green and bright meadow with trees and shrubs. In this meadow was a deer grazing contently and curiously watching me.

The third image was from the first chakra which is centered at the base of the spine. The image appeared quickly. I was astride a large wooly buffalo holding on to its neck and enjoying the warmth and softness of its fur as it grazed contently.

The fourth image was from the second chakra, just below my navel, representing that emotional part of myself. I was sitting in an alley with my legs extended and apart, with a gray rat standing between my legs slightly beyond my feet. A few feet away, against the wall of a building, was a garbage can, new or clean in appearance. The rat was looking at me, and I knew it was asking me for permission to go rummage through the garbage can.

I enjoyed talking about these images with several people over the next twenty-four hours, but again, I was trying too hard to understand them. It was a real pleasure to have Rene as part of my workshop on power struggles. I also spent time reading about the meaning of each chakra in an attempt to uncover a correspondence between the chakra and the points of the medicine wheel. The correspondence is not clear.

In driving home on Sunday, June 18, I found insight. In using the medicine wheel taxonomy, rodents are animals of the South, of trust, playfulness and innocence. The deer and buffalo are animals of the North, or animals of wisdom, understanding and spirituality. In bringing the squirrel and rat together, it struck me that the rat was that garbage or distrusting part of me asking to let go. The squirrel was beckoning me to follow him up the tree of life, the path connecting Mother Earth and Father Sky, to rise above distrust. I told the rat it was free to go. The other images indicated that I felt secure and content in my spirituality, in my wisdom and understanding. Only when I let go of trying too hard to understand did the feeling of these images register and make sense. My struggle with distrust was beginning to be over.

Over the next few weeks I found my anxiety greatly diminished, but even more to my excitement, I found that I was able to talk with physicians and attorneys and feel relaxed, that I could actually enjoy talking with them. I had lost my intimidation of authority; I was finally able to talk with people in authority and trust them.

Notes

FOREWORD

1. Calleman, *The Mayan Calendar and the Transformation of Consciousness,* 56–57.

CHAPTER 1. ECSTATIC TRANCE AND THE MODERN JOURNEYER

1. Gore, *Ecstatic Body Postures,* 4.
2. Goodman, *Speaking in Tongues,* 24–57.
3. Gore, *Ecstatic Body Postures,* 6–8.
4. Ibid., 12.
5. Ibid., 32.
6. Feinstein, "Stories from Your Mystic Depth," 141.
7. Deloria, *The World We Used to Live In,* 15.
8. Mueller, quoted in Gore, *Ecstatic Body Postures,* 12.
9. Ibid., 12.
10. Goodman, *Where the Spirits Ride the Wind,* 25–26.
11. Gore, *Ecstatic Body Postures,* 26.
12. Araoz, *The New Hypnosis,* 4.
13. Jean Gebser, *The Ever-Present Origin.*

CHAPTER 2. THE UNITY OF ECSTATIC EXPERIENCES AND POTENTIAL INFLUENCES

1. Capra, *The Tao of Physics,* 130.
2. Ibid., 131.

3. Capra, *The Tao of Physics,* 130.

4. Sheldrake, *The Presence of the Past,* chapter 7.

5. Capra, *Tao of Physics,* 207–24.

6. Ibid., 211.

CHAPTER 3. INITIATING THE ECSTATIC JOURNEY

1. Mehl-Madrona, *Narrative Medicine,* 234–35.

2. Storm, *Seven Arrows,* 4–11.

3. Waters, *Masked Gods,* 174.

4. Ibid., 175.

CHAPTER 4. THE PURPOSES OF THE ECSTATIC EXPERIENCES

1. Laszlo, *Science and the Akashic Field,* 150.

2. Delora, *The World We Used to Live In,* 68–69.

3. Sheldrake, *The Presence of the Past.*

4. Laszlo, *The Akashic Experience.*

5. Braden, *The Divine Matrix.*

6. Karl Jung, *The Portable Jung.*

CHAPTER 6. DIVINATION POSTURES

1. Gore, *Ecstatic Body Postures,* 111

2. Ibid., 100.

CHAPTER 7. INITIATION POSTURES

1. Gore, *Ecstatic Body Postures,* 221.

2. Ibid., 231.

CHAPTER 8. SPIRIT JOURNEYING AND METAMORPHOSIS POSTURES

1. Gore, *Ecstatic Body Postures,* 206.

2. Ibid., 189–90.

3. Ibid., 199.
4. Goodman, *Where the Spirits Ride the Wind*, 156–57.
5. Gore, *Ecstatic Body Postures*, 144.
6. Ibid., 143–44.

CHAPTER 9. ATTAINING SELF-ACTUALIZATION

1. Gore, *Ecstatic Body Postures*, 109–10.
2. Gore, *The Ecstatic Experience*, 82–83.
3. Gore, *Ecstatic Body Postures*, 195–96.
4. Ibid., 270–71.

CHAPTER 11. CULTIVATING PARAPSYCHOLOGICAL ABILITIES

1. Mitchell, *The Way of the Explorer.*

CHAPTER 12. ACCESSING THE UNIVERSAL MIND

1. Gebser, *The Ever-Present Origin.*
2. Radin, *Entangled Minds*, 284.
3. In Laszlo, *Science and the Akashic Field*, 51.
4. Laszlo, *The Akashic Experience.*
5. Sheldrake, *The Presence of the Past.*
6. Laszlo, *The Akashic Experience*, 76.
7. Laszlo, *Science and the Akashic Field*, 150.
8. Laszlo, *Science and the Akashic Field*, 68–69.
9. Laszlo, *The Akashic Experience*, 250.
10. Waggoner, *Lucid Dreaming*, 79–81.11.
11. Laszlo, *The Akashic Experience*, 130–31.
12. Waggoner, *Lucid Dreaming*, 79.

CONCLUSION. GOING BEYOND

1. Theodore Sarbin, *Narrative Psychology.*
2. Krippner, Bova, and Gray, *Healing Stories.*

3. Mehl-Madrona, *Narrative Medicine.*
4. Brink, *Metaphor Creation for Use Within Family Therapy,* 259.
5. Thompson, *Curiosity of Erickson,* 415.
6. Laszlo, *Science and the Akashic Field,* 150.
7. Mehl-Madrona, *Narrative Medicine.*
8. Bulkeley, *Visions of the Night,* 32.

APPENDIX A. THE HEALING POWERS OF
THE NATIVE AMERICAN MEDICINE WHEEL

1. Eddy, "Probing the Mystery of the Medicine Wheel," 140–46.
2. Storm, *Seven Arrows.*
3. Deer, *Lame Deer Seeker of Visions.*
4. Castaneda, *Tales of Power.*
5. Andrews, *Crystal Woman.*
6. Brink, "Dealing with Traumatic Images"
7. Brink, "Imagery and Family Therapy."
8. Storm, *Seven Arrows;* Andrews, *Flight of the Seventh Moon.*
9. Waters, *Book of the Hopi*
10. Storm, *Seven Arrows.*
11. Deer, *Lame Deer Seeker of Visions.*
12. Andrews, *Medicine Woman.*
13. Harner, *The Way of the Shaman, a Guide to Power and Healing.*
14. Castaneda, *Tales of Power.*
15. Andrews, *Jaguar Woman.*
16. Harner, *The Way of the Shaman.*
17. Desoille, *The Directed Daydream.*
18. Watkins, "The Affect Bridge: A Hypnoanalytic Technique," 21–27.
19. Assogioli, *The Act of Will.*
20. Neihardt, *Black Elk Speaks.*
21. Brink, "Dealing with Traumatic Images."
22. Haley, *Ordeal Therapy.*
23. Watkins, "The Affect Bridge: A Hypnoanalytic Technique," 21–27.
24. Araoz, *The New Hypnosis.*
25. Brink, "Three Stages of Hypno-family Therapy for Psychosomatic Problems."

26. Eugenia Pickett, "Fibroid Tumors and Response to Guided Imagery and Music," 165–76.

27. Andrews, *Jaguar Woman*.

APPENDIX B. TEN DAYS IN JUNE

1. Araoz, *The New Hypnosis.*

2. Baudouin, *Suggestion and Autosuggestion.*

3. Brink, "The Healing Powers of the Native American Medicine Wheel," 45–54.

4. Gallegos, *The Personal Totem Pole, Animal Imagery, the Chakras, and Psychotherapy.*

Bibliography

Andrews, Lynn V. *Crystal Woman.* New York: Warner Books, 1987.

———. *Flight of the Seventh Moon.* New York: Harper & Row, 1984.

———. *Jaguar Woman.* New York: Harper & Row, 1985.

———. *Medicine Woman.* San Francisco: Harper & Row, 1981.

Araoz, Daniel. *The New Hypnosis.* New York: Brunner/Mazel, 1985.

Assogioli, Roberto. *The Act of Will.* London: Wildwood House, 1973.

Baudouin, C. *Suggestion and Autosuggestion.* London: George Allen and Unwin Ltd., 1920

Beowulf, trans. David Wright. New York: Penguin, 1957.

Braden, Gregg. *The Divine Matrix: Bridging Time, Space, Miracles, and Belief.* Carlsbad, Calif.: Hay House, 2007.

Brink, Nicholas E. "Dealing with Traumatic Images." *Bulletin of the American Association of the Study of Mental Imagery* 2, no. 2 (1979): 3–4.

———. "Metaphor Creation for Use Within Family Therapy." *The American Journal of Clinical Hypnosis* 24, no. 4 (1982): 259.

———. *Grendel and His Mother: Healing the Traumas of Childhood through Dreams, Imagery and Hypnosis.* Amityville, N.Y.: Baywood, 2002.

———. "The Healing Powers of the Native American Medicine Wheel." In *Imagery: Current Perspectives,* 45–54. Edited by Joseph E. Shorr, Pennee Robin, Jack A. Connella, and Milton Wolpin. New York: Plenum, 1990.

———. "Imagery and Family Therapy," In *Imagery, Volume 3.* Edited by J. E. Shorr, G. Sobel-Whittington, P. Robin, and J. A. Cannella. New York: Plenum, 1983.

———. "Ten Days in June." *Imagination, Cognition and Personality* 11, no.1 (1991–1992): 99–102.

———. "Three Stages of Hypno-family Therapy for Psychosomatic Problems." *Imagination, Cognition and Personality* 6, no. 3 (1987): 263–70.

Bulkeley, Kelly. *Visions of the Night: Dreams, Religion, and Psychology.* Albany: State University of NY Press, 1999.

Calleman, Carl Johan. *The Mayan Calendar and the Transformation of Consciousness.* Rochester, Vt.: Bear & Co., 2004.

Campbell, Jean. *Group Dreaming: Dreams to the Tenth Power.* Norfolk, Va.: Wordminder Press, 2006.

Capra, Fritjof. *Tao of Physics: An Exploration of the Parallels between Modern Physics and Eastern Mysticism.* Boston: Shambhala, 2000.

Castenada, Carlos. *Tales of Power.* New York: Pocket Books, 1974.

———. *The Teachings of Don Juan: A Yaqui Way of Knowledge.* Berkeley: University of California Press, 1968.

Deer, John Fire Lame, and Richard Erdoes. *Lame Deer Seeker of Visions.* New York: Pocket Books, 1972.

Deloria Jr., Vine. *The World We Used to Live In: Remembering the Powers of the Medicine Men.* Golden, Colo.: Fulcrum, 2006.

Desoille, R. *The Directed Daydream.* New York: Psychosynthesis Research Foundation, 1966.

Eddy, J. A. "Probing the Mystery of the Medicine Wheel." *National Geographic* 151, no. 1 (1977): 140–46.

Feinstein, David. "Stories from Your Mystic Depth." In *Healing Stories: The Use of Narrative in Counseling and Psychotherapy,* edited by Stanley Krippner, Michael Bova, and Leslie Gray. Charlottesville, Va.: Puente, Publications, 2007.

Gallegos, E. S. *The Personal Totem Pole, Animal Imagery, the Chakras, and Psychotherapy.* Santa Fe, N.M.: Moon Bear Press, 1987.

Gebser, Jean. *The Ever-Present Origin.* Trans. Noel Barstad. Athens, Oh.: Ohio University Press, 1953.

Goodman, Felicitas. *Speaking in Tongues: A Cross-Cultural Study of Glossolalia.* Chicago: University of Chicago Press, 1972.

———. *Where the Spirits Ride the Wind: Trance Journeys and Other Ecstatic Experiences.* Bloomington, Ind.: Indiana University Press, 1990.

Gore, Belinda. *Ecstatic Body Postures: An Alternate Reality Workbook.* Rochester, Vt.: Bear & Co., 1995.

———. *The Ecstatic Experience: Healing Postures for Spirit Journeys.* Rochester, Vt.: Bear & Co., 2009.

Haley, Jay. *Ordeal Therapy*. San Francisco: Jossey-Bass, 1984.

Harner, Michael. *The Way of the Shaman: A Guide to Power and Healing*. New York: Bantam Books, 1986.

Jung, Karl. *The Portable Jung*. Trans. R. F. C. Hull. New York: Viking, 1971.

Krippner, Stanley, Michael Bova, and Leslie Gray, eds. *Healing Stories: The Use of Narrative in Counseling and Psychotherapy*. Charlottesville, Va.: Puente, Publications, 2007.

Laszlo, Ervin. *The Akashic Experience: Science and the Cosmic Memory Field*. Rochester, Vt.: Inner Traditions, 2009.

———. *Science and the Akashic Field: An Integral Theory of Everything*. Rochester, Vt.: Inner Traditions, 2007.

Mehl-Madrona, Lewis, and Thom Hartmann. *Healing the Mind Through the Power of Story: The Promise of Narrative Psychiatry*. Rochester, Vt.: Bear & Co., 2010.

———. *Narrative Medicine: The Use of History and Story in the Healing Process*. Rochester, Vt.: Bear & Co., 2007.

Mitchell, Edgar R. *The Way of the Explorer: An Apollo Astronaut's Journey through the Material and Mystical Worlds*. New York: Putnam, 1996.

Neihardt, J. G. *Black Elk Speaks*. New York: Pocket Books, 1932.

Pickett, Eugenia. "Fibroid Tumors and Response to Guided Imagery and Music: Two Case Studies." *Imagination, Cognition and Personality* 7, no. 2 (1988): 165–76.

Playfair, Guy. *Twin Telepathy: The Psychic Connection*. London: Vega Books, 2002.

Popol Vuh: The Mayan Book of the Dawn of Life. Trans. Dennis Tedlock. New York: Simon & Schuster, 1996.

Prechtel, Martin. *Secrets of the Talking Jaguar*. Berkeley, Calif.: North Atlantic Books, 1998.

Radin, Dean. *Entangled Minds: Extrasensory Experiences in a Quantum Reality*. New York: Paraview Pocket Books, 2006.

Sarbin, Theodore. *Narrative Psychology: The Storied Nature of Human Conduct*. Westport, Conn.: Praeger, 1986.

Sheldrake, Rupert. *The Presence of the Past: Morphic Resonance and the Habits of Nature*. Rochester, Vt.: Park Street Press, 1995.

Siegel, Bernie S. *Love, Medicine and Miracles: Lessons Learned about Self-Healing from a Surgeon's Experience with Exceptional Patients*. New York: Harper & Row, 1986.

Simonton, Carl O., M.D. *Getting Well Again: A Step-by-Step, Self-Help Guide to Overcoming Cancer for Patients and Their Families.* Los Angeles: Tarcher, 1978.

Storm, Hyemeyohsts. *Seven Arrows.* New York: Harper & Row, 1985.

Shorr, Joseph E., Pennee Robin, Jack A. Connella, Milton Wolpin. *In Imagery: Current Perspectives.* New York: Plenum Press, 1989.

Sturluson, Snorri. *The Prose Edda.* Trans. Jean Young. Berkeley: University of California Press, 1954.

Thompson, Kay. "Curiosity of Erickson." In *Ericksonian Approaches to Hypnosis and Psychotherapy.* Edited by J. K. Zeig. New York: Brunner/Mazel, 1982.

Waggoner, Robert. *Lucid Dreaming: Gateway to the Inner Self.* Needham, Mass.: Moment Point Press, 2009.

Waters, Frank. *Book of the Hopi.* New York: Penguin Books, 1963.

———. *Masked Gods: Navaho and Pueblo Ceremonialism.* Athens, Oh.: Swallow Press, 1950.

Watkins, John G. "The Affect Bridge: A Hypnoanalytic Technique." *Journal of Clinical Hypnosis* 19 (1971): 21–27.

Wilson, Ian. *The After Death Experience: The Physics of the Non-Physical.* New York: William Morrow and Company, 1987.

Index

Page numbers in *italics* refer to illustrations.

BOOKS OF RELATED INTEREST

The Ecstatic Experience
Healing Postures for Spirit Journeys
by Belinda Gore

Ecstatic Body Postures
An Alternate Reality Workbook
by Belinda Gore

Ecstatic Healing
A Journey into the Shamanic World of Spirit Possession
and Miraculous Medicine
by Margaret De Wys

Shaking Medicine
The Healing Power of Ecstatic Movement
by Bradford Keeney

Shamanic Breathwork
Journeying beyond the Limits of the Self
by Linda Star Wolf

Seven Secrets of Time Travel
Mystic Voyages of the Energy Body
by Von Braschler

Shapeshifting
Techniques for Global and Personal Transformation
by John Perkins

Net of Being
by Alex Grey with Allyson Grey

INNER TRADITIONS • BEAR & COMPANY
P.O. Box 388
Rochester, VT 05767
1-800-246-8648
www.InnerTraditions.com

Or contact your local bookseller